BE A TRAVEL WRITER, LIVE YOUR DREAMS, SELL YOUR FEATURES

An inspirational and motivational journey through the world of travel writing.

Be a Travel Writer is your transportation of choice to your destination of published travel writer. It draws upon Solange's expert knowledge as she shares tips and tricks learned in the course of her career.

Climb aboard, for a whole new world of discovery awaits you.
Simon Whaley, best selling author, feature writer and photographer, member of the Outdoor Writers and Photographers Guild

If anyone knows how to write and sell travel features, it is Solange Hando. She is so right that the rewards are tremendous and as she says, every experience is packed with article ideas.

This great little book brims with her valuable advice, encouragement and insider's knowledge, from travel basics to professional expertise.
Andrew Sanger, award-winning travel writer, editor and guide book author

Be a Travel Writer, Live your Dreams, Sell your Features

Travel Writing Step by Step

Be a Travel Writer, Live your Dreams, Sell your Features

Travel Writing Step by Step

Solange Hando

**COMPASS
BOOKS**

Winchester, UK
Washington, USA

First published by Compass Books, 2014
Compass Books is an imprint of John Hunt Publishing Ltd., Laurel House, Station Approach,
Alresford, Hants, SO24 9JH, UK
office1@jhpbooks.net
www.johnhuntpublishing.com
www.compass-books.net

For distributor details and how to order please visit the 'Ordering' section on our website.

Text copyright: Solange Hando 2013

ISBN: 978 1 78099 944 9

A CIP catalogue record for this book is available from the British Library.

Design: Lee Nash

Printed and bound by CPI Group (UK) Ltd, Croydon, CR0 4YY

We operate a distinctive and ethical publishing philosophy in all
areas of our business, from our global network of authors to
production and worldwide distribution.

CONTENTS

To Sidney, William, Felicia and Isabella
so they may live their dreams, whatever they may be.

Acknowledgments

I would like to thank Cherry Cuckoo, Della Galton and Pamela Spencer for their feedback, Kathryn Burrington, Stuart Forster, Ashley Gibbins, Lynne Hackles, Linda Jackson and Mari Nicholson for their contributions and all the tutors, editors, colleagues and family members who have encouraged me over the years.

Works by Solange Hando

Contributing author:

National Geographic: Journeys of a Lifetime, Food Journeys, Sacred places, Secret Places, Where the Locals Go

Quintessence: 1001 Escapes

Reader's Digest: Best of the Best Places in the World

Worth Press Ltd: Paris Memories of Times Past

Travel journalist:

Wide range of features published in 96 titles worldwide

Introduction

"See it, Believe it, Do it"

Travel writing? Brilliant! Seeing the world, getting paid, where do you start? You took the first step when you opened this book. It will point you in the right direction but don't dream of a free vacation just yet. Wait until you've reached the last page. The truth is that travel writers are never on vacation. They get up at dawn, rush around making notes and taking pictures then spend the evening at their laptop. It's hard work but it is a wonderful life and the more effort you put in, the greater the reward.

Are you ready for the challenge? Do you love traveling, exploring, hovering here and there like a butterfly? Would you like to share your adventures and earn some cash along the way?

You've come to the right place

Travel features are short-term projects, a gift for busy people. Each one claims only a few hours of your time, a couple of days at most, leaving you free to travel, enjoy life and fit in other commitments. They can be as varied and exciting as you wish, perfect for fluttering minds and travelers on the move.

Hop on a plane, hire a bike, relax in a spa and when you come home, write a feature or two and re-live the experience. Twice the pleasure, but this time it's free. Get it right and an editor will buy.

Let's get creative

Travel writing is creative. Don't let anyone tell you otherwise. Words are your tools and like a painter's palette, how you use them reflects your personality and view of the world. You and I could visit the same place, have the same experience yet describe it in a totally different way.

Be yourself, write about your passion, share your stories with family, colleagues and friends but best of all, see your name in print, your words and pictures on the page, or on the web, as you entertain and inform readers from every sphere of life. Sounds good?

Simple skills for everyone
This book will lead you step by step on the road to publication from early planning and research to photography, from ideas and style to pleasing editors so they will buy your work. Begin to build your portfolio, learn where and how to network and you will realize that the old adage comes true: *"Success Breeds Success."*

There will be a few ups and downs. I have them too but let's call them challenges and enjoy. Like most things in life, determination wins in the end.

Why features?
Let me share a secret: I started with a book. It was turned down 36 times but a kind publisher pointed out great potential for features, a dozen or more, if I got it right. I took the advice and never looked back.

So for most of us, regardless of age, purpose or destination, new to the trade or published in a different field, writing features is the easiest way to break into the genre. Gap year, family vacation, grand tour of Europe, culture fan, adventurer or beach lover, every experience is packed with article ideas.

Better still, travel does not have to be exotic, it's about people and places and this is wherever you are, New York, the Scottish Highlands, Australia or your own backyard. Home to you is travel to someone else.

Any special requirements?
Here's the list:

Do You Enjoy

- Discovering places?
- Meeting people?
- Learning new things?

Can You

- Write in simple English?
- Take digital pictures?

Are You

- Determined, 100 per cent?
- Hard-working, most of the time?
- Reasonably organized?
- Eager to step up and give this your best?

Writing is the last step to publication.

- Are you prepared to learn before you jump?

Mostly 'yes'?
Excellent, fasten your seatbelt, we're ready to go.

Welcome Aboard

Planning for Success

"A journey of a thousand miles begins with a single step."
Lao Tzu, Chinese philosopher

When was your last holiday?
    What did you do?
    What was your favorite place or activity?
    Why?
    If you are on the road, recall your most recent experience.
    Would you like to write about it and get paid?
That's what I do and if I can, anyone can. You don't need formal qualifications in media studies but give it a couple of years and you could be selling dozens of features worldwide.
    What is the secret?

Believe in yourself.
Do your research.

Imagine an entrepreneur planning to start a business.
    What's the first step?
    Market research: location, prospective clients, their expectations and how to satisfy them.
    Travel writing is no different.

Research your market, make your choice, tailor your writing and you will succeed, sooner rather than later.

The Big World of Travel Features

Guess how many English magazines are published around the world? Millions every year, with an average of 2600 copies sold every minute in the UK, according to industry data, spread across a huge range of titles, not counting newspapers and websites.

Add North America, Australia, New Zealand, plus another 80 countries or so where English is an official language, and you may feel overwhelmed by the volume of global outlets. This covers all kinds of magazines but most feature travel of some sort.

True, publications do vanish overnight but next time you hear of a shrinking market, remember that in this digital age, the world is yours.

Choosing wisely

Most consumer magazines appear weekly or monthly. A weekly publication will need 52 articles a year for a travel page and more for special editions. That's a lot of space to fill. A monthly will probably use 12 features during that time so every submission must be outstanding. Meanwhile, most newspapers publish several travel pieces in their weekly slot, plus a generous crop in weekend supplements. You do the math. Quality matters, numbers too.

But how about those gorgeous travel magazines filling their entire copy with features like yours? Tempting but like most glossies, they aim upmarket. A famous name on the cover, say Bill Bryson or Michael Palin, is sure to draw attention and boost sales. The higher you climb, the stiffer the competition but don't despair. Everything is possible if you have an original idea and the right approach.

Searching every corner of the market

Titles come and go but the lure of travel remains; the range of outlets continues to grow.

Where do we begin?

- Travel magazines: note that each one has its own slant, backpacking, luxury, adventure, eco-tourism, or covers a specific destination, such as Italy or the Caribbean.
- Newspapers, travel pages and supplements, national, regional and local.
- In-flight magazines: most carry features in English, relating to new routes or topical events on existing routes, including those of partner airlines.
- Magazines issued by railway or cruise companies, highlighting places of interest along their routes or ports of call.
- Women's magazines, most have a travel or travel related page.
- Men's magazines, but you don't have to be a man to write for them, or the reverse.
- Lifestyle: health, property, spa, cruising, weddings and honeymoon, spiritual matters.
- Publications targeting a specific age or social group: families, over 50s, gay, singles, religious communities, business travelers, disabled travelers, farmers, teachers, nurses.
- Publications about sports and outdoors, golf, cycling, hiking, scuba diving...
- Niche markets, such as bird watching, art, crafts, food and wine, heritage, vintage railways, gardens, antiques and even pets.
- County or regional magazines.
- Trade magazines published by hotel chains, tour operators, banks, stores or car dealers, plus online content and travel anthologies by National Geographic or Reader's Digest.

Out of breath? That's a good sign for now you know.

In the big world of travel features, there's a place for you.

Here are useful resources to help you find it; most require a subscription but they list many publications beyond those at local newsstands:

- www.awmonline.com.au (Australia)
- www.woodenhorsepub.com (North America)
- www.writersmarket.com (USA)
- www.writersandartists.co.uk (UK)
- www.world-newspapers.com (worldwide)

Now your turn

- Choose a time and a place and promise yourself you will spend at least 30 minutes looking at magazines, this week and the next. Don't read cover to cover at this stage, scan titles and pictures and something will catch your eye.
- Perhaps there's a travel page you read every week. Is it in a paper or a magazine? Why do you like it? Is it the photographs, style, content? If you enjoy a publication, you empathize with its readers and writing for them will come naturally. It's a great place to start.
- Let your confidence grow and when you're ready, venture out of your comfort zone, new markets at home, foreign publications on the web, some offering free trial subscriptions, others contributors' guidelines.

Top tips

1. Being aware of a publication isn't enough, you must study who the readers are and what they want. We will cover this in step 7 but if you're in the mood right now, give it a go. Open any magazine and spot the clues.
2. Always look out for new publications and editors, get in touch before they've set up their regular contributors' list.

Congratulate new editors on their appointment when you send your pitch.

3. When you begin, don't reject a magazine because it is obscure or pays poor rates, you never know who might spot your work. All exposure is good whether it's print, online or word of mouth.

4. Keep an open mind and don't judge anything by its cover:

"Did you see this?" asked one of my students, pointing to a double-page spread in a celebrity magazine.
"Wow, the Living Goddess of Kathmandu? I could have done that."

Why didn't I? Celebrities aren't my patch. I'd never looked at the magazine but beyond the gossip, I discovered a travel slot with a difference. I learned my lesson. People stories are in demand, child labour in India, women porters in Nepal and more, published within months.

Getting a Head Start

If you are planning to write about your last trip, that's fine and I'll show you how. But next time round, get ahead of the game. Before you go, ask yourself what kind of travel is in vogue, which destinations, activities or means of transport. Spot the trends, bear them in mind wherever you go and you will increase your chance of success.

"But stop," I hear you say, "does this mean I can't be myself?" Not at all, we are all individuals, we all have our own voice but if we want our work to be published, there is no room for self-indulgence. Readers come first. It's a hard lesson to learn but do it and you will succeed.

New interests

Vacations are getting more sophisticated. We're looking for a break but if we are to part with our cash, we want more than dozing on the beach ten hours a day. Most of us prefer to be active, at least some of the time, pursuing an interest, learning a skill or saving the planet.

On the rise:

- Green holidays: visiting national parks and reserves; volunteering to save turtles or orang-utans; seeking eco-friendly venues from farm houses to award-winning resorts; carbon-free travel, rail journeys, cycling, walking.
- Short breaks: 2 to 5 nights, short or medium haul, accessed by low cost flight or high speed rail.
- Cruising: open sea or inland waterways.
- Activity holidays: anything from white water rafting to painting or soft adventure.
- Gastronomy: gourmet vacations, wine tours, cookery schools.
- Off the beaten track: remote mountains or islands, barely discovered countries or hidden gems in well-known places.
- Body and soul: spa, retreats, meditation, yoga.
- Real estate: buying a place in the sun.
- Medical tourism: dentistry, cosmetic surgery, sex change and routine operations.

Which of these trends would appeal to you?

Take note and remember them when you plan a vacation.

New places

Have you noticed how a destination suddenly appears in lots of publications at the same time? This is rarely a coincidence but the likely result of a promotional campaign by the tourist board, often prompted by topical factors.

Trend spotters?

Full steam ahead, this is what to look for:

- End of hostilities or sanctions: reopening a country to responsible tourism and safe travel.
- Destinations freshly recovered from a natural disaster, attracting visitors with special offers.
- Emerging destinations benefiting from new investments in infrastructure.
- World sports events.
- Awards: Top Green City, Capital of Culture or Sports, newly granted UNESCO status.
- Topical events, royal wedding, visit by a Head of State.
- News items bringing a country or theme into the limelight.
- Up and downturns in the economy, in particular the exchange rate which can make a destination highly attractive or place it out of most people's reach.

How do I know what's happening?

As soon as a trend is obvious, everyone has covered it so try to keep abreast of forthcoming developments.

Think 'travel' when you listen to the news. Search the web, attend travel shows, collect the latest travel brochures from tour operators and study their adverts for new destinations and products.

Most importantly, contact the CVB (convention and visitors bureau) or tourist board of places you intend to visit, introduce yourself as a travel writer and ask to be placed on their mailing list.

Old favorites? New approach

Does this mean your planned vacation to Florida won't sell?

Absolutely not for places change all the time and there's always a new way of looking at them. Your job is to find it.

The following hot spots have been covered extensively but still offered scope to savvy writers:

Florence: what is it like to wander through the city streets after dark? Feature: Evenings in Florence.

The Taj Mahal: disaster, it's raining when you get there. Feature: The Taj Mahal in the rain.

Ireland: something different? Feature: Learning to cook in Dublin.

Now your turn

Think of a vacation, past or future, or your own neighborhood:

- Anything new or unusual?
- Anything you could approach in an original way?
- Can you come up with at least one idea?

Write it down and follow up within a week, this could be the start of your career as a travel writer.

Top tips

1. If you're thinking 'global markets', keep up to date with destinations likely to attract local readers and advertisers. Mexico is popular in North America but how about Bali or Japan? These could be easier to sell in Australasia while the UK tends to lean towards southern Europe.
2. If you have a great interview however, or a heart-rending story, it will find its way around the world, regardless of location. Act quickly and collect the rewards. Multiple sales are every writer's dream.

Researching your Trip

Are you easy going or super organized?
Do you book your vacation months in advance?
Do you always pack more than you need?
Do you double check your reservations, plus one more time for luck?
Do you read a guide book or research on the web before you go?
Do you decide exactly what you'll do when you get there?
Do you read reviews?
Do you consider the weather before you book?

Mostly 'yes', you are super organized, well done.
Mostly 'no', you are easy going and that's just as good:

Plan before you go, adapt when you're there.

Will planning take the fun out of your trip?
Not in the least, half the pleasure of traveling is anticipation. A plan simply opens your eyes to possibilities. There will be plenty more along the way.

Things to see and do? Make a list
Lists are powerful. They make us feel good when we tick things off and they free the mind. Don't worry about remembering this or that, keep your list safe and it will do it all for you.

Go through your guide book, the websites, any information collected from tourism authorities, travel shows or agents and write down your A list, sights you want to see, things you want to do.

Pay attention to anything specific or unique to the country: an artist colony in St Lucia, Kew Gardens in London, the Erotic Museum in Paris or watching the sunset on Ayres Rock.

Remember the trends and your market research: should you look for real estate, medical care, theme parks, heritage sites? Gather as much information as possible and aim to sell at least three features for every trip. You will be paid to write, not to travel.

How many days do you have, seven?

This was my schedule in Costa Rica:

Day 1: Explore Poas volcano and national park

Day 2: Visit Gold Museum and tourist sites in San Jose

Day 3: Bird watching on Tarcoles river

Day 4: Street food, local market and fishing harbor

Day 5: Bathe in Arenal hot springs, visit Tabacon hotel

Day 6: Hike in cloud forest

Day 7: Head for Sarchi, research local craft, interview artisans

Seven days, seven features, plus a hotel review. Sell half of them and you're well on your way to make it pay.

But why not decide on arrival, you may ask? You'll probably spend the first day recovering from the journey and the next deciding where to start. You're ready on day three but on day four, you realize you missed the eco-farm, you ought to retrace your steps but you don't have time. All it takes is a little planning and when your list is ready, prioritize and group your activities in a logical way.

A working trip is not a vacation but don't go to extremes, especially if money is a bonus rather than a priority. It's fine to combine business and leisure, what matters most is enjoyment. Have fun, relax and it will show in your writing.

Practicalities? Get them right

Have you ever gone to a village and missed the festival by a day?

What happened last night? Sounds so mysterious, everybody's whispering about it.

"Wow, madame, it was the naked dance, all the men do it. They cover their face, nothing else, and all the ladies come to watch. They try to guess who's who, there's a lot of giggling and sometimes, well, they get it wrong..., shame you missed it, maybe you come back next year?"

If I do, I'll check the dates.

Festivals aside, here are a few things to look for before you go:

- Opening times and days of cultural sites, businesses, spas, restaurants you might want to review.
- Public holidays: transport tends be scarce or non-existent.
- Market days, when and where.
- Anniversaries providing a topical hook for your feature during the current year or the next.
- Seasonal patterns at your destination, perhaps you don't mind the rain but monsoon storms often cause havoc with travel plans and most magazines prefer blue skies on their travel page. Will there be blossom on the trees, penguins on the beach, locals in summer dress or winter coats? Think ideas and pictures. What will it be like?
- Current prices of food, accommodation, car rental, hidden charges and taxes so you don't run out of budget and are forced to skip something you wanted to do.
- Areas to avoid: getting into trouble might make a good story but you'll have to survive to tell the tale.

Local sensitivities? Respect them
Your most original material is likely to involve local people. Show respect and you will gain their trust. On an escorted tour, the guide will brief you, but if you travel on your own, be aware of the 'do' and 'don't' beforehand.

Consider the following points:

- Dress code when visiting religious places but also in cities and on the beach.
- Colors, is white for weddings or funerals?
- Etiquette in a local home, what guests can and cannot do.
- Eating and drinking, is it alright to use your left hand, offer food from your plate?
- Interacting with children, monks, village leaders.
- Giving and receiving gifts, how to, why they don't say 'thank you'.
- Taking photographs, ethics, people or places to avoid.
- Taboos, such as pointing with your index finger, eye contact for women or displays of affection in public.

Top tips

1. Source a local contact before you travel:
   Ask friends or family and get in touch with the tourist board. How about your local clubs, associations, charities, anything from Rotary or Lions to a writers' circle? Do they have links abroad? How about a visit, an interview?
   Introduce yourself as a writer rather than a journalist. The latter might arouse suspicion.
2. Learn a few words of the language, it will go a long way towards breaking the ice.
   'Hello, thank you, what is your name, how are you,' are sure to bring a smile, followed by a hearty chuckle when you're thrown out of your depth. Share a laugh and you might be asked in for a cup of tea or a glass of chang beer. Worth the effort, isn't it?
   Don't forget sign language, nodding can mean 'no', shrugging shoulders can mean 'yes'.
3. Pack small gifts.
   Think what locals would appreciate, cheap for you but useful or precious for them, a bar of scented soap in the

depth of Africa, a postcard of the Dalai Lama for a Tibetan exile, pens for school kids in a Colombian village. Hand out your gift to the teacher, the mother who invited you into her home, the self-appointed guide who took you to a village party with not a tourist in sight.

4. Book a window seat on the plane on the side with the best views. Seeing your new destination from the air is exciting and first impressions do matter.

Still with us?

Brilliant, let's move on to the next stage...

Step 2

On the Road

"Travel is like love..., a heightened state of awareness in which we are mindful, receptive, undimmed by familiarity and ready to be transformed."
Pico Iyer, author

Should you rely on organized tours or go it alone?

Tours have limitations but if you are short of time, it's probably the best option: no need to queue at the station or the palace gate, everything is pre-arranged. On a longer stay, it's a good way to get your bearings before you set off on your own. I love wandering as I please but rely on a local guide, preferably self-appointed, to show me the real thing.

Keeping a Diary

Time on the road is precious. You don't want to spend daylight hours scribbling away or glued to a laptop. But with so much to see, so much to do, how will you remember it all? Easy. Use an audio-recorder but don't babble on for hours. Listening back will take time. Alternatively, carry a small note pad and jot down a few words, enough to jog your memory when you knuckle down to work, late at night or before breakfast. Pink blossom on town square, monkey licking tap, offerings in temple (rice, marigolds), pig on motorbike.

This leaves you free to explore and allows you to be discreet. Scribbling away in public is sure to draw attention, which you may not want, and could endanger your safety in certain quarters. Besides, should you forget your pad on a bench, it won't be the end of the world.

It's a much bigger problem if you lose a full diary, the most precious tool of any travel writer. Make sure everything on a laptop is backed up and if you use a conventional notebook, keep it safe and write an address or phone number on the first page in case it goes astray.

Perhaps we'll use only 10 or 20 per cent of our notes but what matters is having them in case we need them. We probably will at some point. Some subjects are evergreen as long as you update from time to time.

A word of warning: think twice before recording controversial matter in a diary or otherwise. Your bag could be searched at a checkpoint and get you or others in trouble. Keep your notes safe and seemingly neutral so only you can read between the lines. Use your imagination.

Facts for your diary

A diary isn't a guide book but most travel writers are expected to provide some useful information to their readers. Save this in a dedicated file in your laptop or use the back of your journal, so when you read through, the nitty-gritty won't interfere with the flow. Annotate as you go along, using italics, bold, underlining, color coding, so it's easier to spot the relevant section.

Points to bear in mind:

- Double check any research you did at home, prices, opening times, especially if you used a guide book, two years in the making. In this fast changing world, even the web lags behind.
- Note names of villages, rivers, plants, trees, birds. The local language will do, translate later.
- Names of people, guides, children, villagers you meet. If you have only one or two local names, jot down a few more, male and female, and add them to your list. They could come in handy.
- Distances: mileage but also the time it takes to cover the

distance, whether you're hiking in the Andes or boarding a bullet train in Japan.

- If you intend reviewing a hotel, compile a fact file.
- Write down email addresses and phone numbers of tourist boards, guides and people you meet in case you want to contact them at a later date.

Getting personal

Facts are essential but they won't make your writing stand out from the pile. Your own reactions to people and places, your feelings and observations will reveal your personality and make a difference. Learn to be observant, develop an eye for detail and practice until it becomes second nature.

Do you have a reliable local guide? Good, listen for interesting quotes and anecdotes but don't write down what you can read online or copy the information on a poster, take a photograph. Scan the scene, jot down what you notice, an erotic carving on a grave, a child with a cell phone in an African hut, anything quirky or unexpected. Learn to multitask: look around, ask questions, take pictures and write brief notes.

Be aware of your senses for that's how you experience the world. Include them in your story and it will come alive as readers visualize what it's like to soak in the sun on a Mexican beach or travel through the Canadian Rockies.

- Notice colors around you: start with the dominant color, blue and white on a Greek island, green in Bali, then note what people wear, the color of rooftops, houses, city walls, temples and churches, the shades of green in the forest, the rivers, blue, silver, brown, the birds, the ocean, the flowers, the food.
- Listen to sounds: traffic, water, people, dogs, bells, the wind in the trees, steel drums beating through the night. What is it like for you? What will you remember most?

- Feel the Khmer silk, the strings of a Spanish guitar, the rough skin of an elephant, the curling leaves of a mimosa plant, the smooth flesh of a dragon fruit. Was it as you imagined?
- Check out where the locals eat: head for the night market in Hong Kong, the floating gardens on Inle Lake, the mobile kitchens in Marrakesh, the sidewalk cafes in Paris.
- Note the smells: sweet, pungent, acrid, subtle, overpowering. Think about jasmine, incense, goats, babies, marigolds, anything that seems to encompass the spirit of a place.
- Note every anecdote, the taxi-cab with no speedometer or fuel gauge, the monkey rubbing his nose on your window as you showered, blissfully unaware.

Top tips

1. Talk to other travelers, perhaps they noticed something you didn't, but check any facts they give you. The same applies to locals, they should know more than you do but go and see for yourself.
2. Collect brochures, postcards, souvenirs, any visual aid that will help recall the atmosphere when you are back at your desk thousands of miles away.
3. Record the sounds mentioned in your diary, schoolchildren learning by rote, chanting monks, bird song, market hawkers. I once taped a flute seller in Kathmandu but with so much noise around, I wished I'd bought a CD. I was glad I didn't. At home, in familiar surroundings, I was carried straight back to the temple square, dogs barking, children screaming, cars honking and in the middle of it all, the plaintive call of a bamboo flute. Just like the real thing.
4. Notice the posters on the walls, read the local paper. Find

out what's happening and what people are talking about, greening the town or the opening of the first luxury hotel. Save cuttings, ask the tourist board for details. Is there potential for a feature or interview?

5. As you write up the day's events, new ideas will almost certainly spring to mind. Don't let them slip away, make notes and if a title comes up, add it to your list of possible features.

Now your turn

- Take a walk around the block, 30 minutes will do, and spot something you've never noticed.
- Remember the five senses and write at least one sentence for each one.

No excuses, there will be something, keep looking and you'll find it.

- Repeat the exercise once a week as you explore places close to home but off your usual route. That's the best way to sharpen your senses and observation skills, ready for adventure.

Going Native

If you want your writing to be convincing, be prepared to try things out, though how brave you are is up to you. You might not want to jump through burning hay in Bhutan to purify your soul but you can get close enough to shudder as your hair begins to singe. You'll understand how it feels but if you stand across the field, you won't.

Do as the locals do: go to church, attend a soccer match, shop in the bazaar, spin a prayer wheel, feed the goldfish for luck.

Join in and record the experience in every detail, what is

happening, how the people are dressed, how they behave, how you feel. Does anyone stand out of the crowd, how? Do you notice anything striking, unusual? The policeman sleeping under a tree, the girl in white hat and gloves shelling peas on the sidewalk, the holy man chasing the cobra which escaped from his basket? These will be the juiciest morsels in your copy.

Taste that food

"Fried spiders, madame? Favorite snack in Cambodia... I've got fat ones and spindly ones, long legs really nice. See this little one, crunchy like a prawn, you try?"

I close my eyes, imagine it's pink, fresh from the sea, and down it goes, reluctantly. I buy a bagful...for the guide.

Now will you order the snake soup or the sheep's eyes? Even one mouthful will be better than none. You'll be pleasantly surprised or you won't, but either way you'll have something to write about.

Watch, taste, ask questions, sample the best aphrodisiac or the local firewater, speak to the cook, the waiter, and you'll be well versed in one of the most trendy topics in travel writing.

But don't be foolhardy, you don't want a day out of action. Keep to hot food, preferably cooked in front of you, and when a newly-acquired friend offers you something suspicious, look a little drab and nurse your stomach, they'll understand.

Sing, dance and be merry
It's festival time.

Here's a tourist: standing on a balcony, camera at the ready, zooming down on the street, trying to pick out the best shot, getting hot and flustered because someone gets in the way, heading back into the room to slump in a chair, closing the window to keep out the noise.

Here's a real traveler: he's done the balcony scene, now he's down in the street, doing whatever the people do, running, dancing, helping to shoulder a shrine on its way to chapel or getting drenched in red powder during the Indian Holi. He vanishes in the crowds, he's one of them.

Which would you be?

Which one would write the most interesting story?

Don't be shy, jump in and if you feel concerned, get a local to look after you. Keep on the edge of the crowd, be prepared for a bit of dirt, water, a bump or two and you'll have a story to sell. It's action, it's real and editors love it.

Dress local, lend a hand

Kira, pins, belt, it was all there, beautifully laid out on the bed, but how do you put on a Bhutanese dress? Perhaps the hotel staff could help?

"Sorry, madam, too early, no ladies on duty."

There I was in a hotel room, 5.30 in the morning, with two men I'd never met, struggling with meters of fabric, red and gold, folding this way, that way, under the arm, over the arm to no avail. "I can't be late for a Coronation," I pleaded, so the youngest ran out into the street to look for a woman, any woman, who might know what to do.

Going native can land you in a twist but if it adds humor or drama to your feature, it's worthwhile. Besides, it often helps to blend in. If everyone wears black and you wear red, you'll stand out; if your golden hair blows freely in the breeze but others wear the veil, you'll draw attention but if a local says 'you look as if you live here', it's the best compliment you could get. It means you can be trusted and that goes a long way towards securing an original story. But don't be alarmed, I won't suggest you strip naked or put on a kira.

Or maybe you could lend a hand? Helping the child scrubbing dishes with mud, giving a 20 minute English lesson in a village school, carrying water from the pump, having a go at winnowing rice or picking grapes at harvest time?

So let's practice at home. Will you wear a fancy dress for Halloween? Will you help to clear a footpath or set up a stall at the next charity event?

The more you get involved, the better the results for travel writing isn't just about places, it's also about people. Remember Paul Theroux' famous line in *The Great Railway Bazaar*: "I sought trains, I found passengers."

Top tips

1. Be flexible and seize the unexpected.

   This is your last day, you planned to visit a temple but someone invites you to share a wedding feast, mountain potatoes glowing in the embers.

   Perhaps you don't like potatoes but which experience will be the most exciting?

   Which one is most likely to impress an editor and entertain readers?

   Be on the lookout, do something different and your writing will reap the rewards.

2. Be ready to explore and get lost within reason. Your best stories are likely to pop up when you stray off the beaten track. Keep to safe areas then a cell phone, taxi number, hotel card and a map should get you back in one piece. If you must ask for directions, keep to open questions, 'which way to..,' and use your common sense.

3. Travel on local transport, at least some of the time. It's often painfully slow but you can't beat it for atmosphere, oranges rolling out of shopping baskets, a live chicken under your seat, legs dangling in front of the window as

lads hitch a ride on the roof. You can't see the view but who cares? It's all happening inside, sights, sounds and smells, the essence of travel writing.

Hop on a train, a ferry, a street car, a rickshaw, a motorbike if you dare, then you will gain a real insider's view, but have directions at hand in the local script. Bus 36? No problem, except I couldn't read Thai.

4. Kids? Showing you where to go, teaching you a few words and sometimes playing tricks. I once walked around a village greeting everyone with a beaming smile and the rudest word on the island. Trust them at your peril.

But now, let's get talking...

Real Life

"When people talk, listen completely. Most people never listen."
Ernest Hemingway

People stories are in demand, usually well paid and relatively easy to write. Talk to a volunteer in Zambia or a zoo keeper in Berlin and they'll provide the content, all you have to do is edit. Does this sound too good to be true? You're right, there's a lot of hard work to put in beforehand.

Travel writers are lucky though. They can arrange formal interviews then discover all sorts of unexpected opportunities along the way. Learn to recognize them and you double your chance of earning cash. Readers always like to know what people get up to, famous or not, as long as it's interesting.

Tell me, how did you end up in a Chinese jail?
    "Well there was a hill with a castle on the top so I decided to go up and take some pictures. Then I spotted a man following me, waving his arms, Sir, Sir, he shouted. Wants to sell me something, I thought, so the faster he walked, the quicker I went until I reached the gate. That's when I realized...'

Make a Date

Arrange formal interviews through contacts at the planning stage. Celebrities welcome publicity, providing you have the right commission upfront, but the ordinary folk among us are less confident. 'I want to write about you' scares people off, tell them you'd like to talk about their work, their hobby, what it's like to live in Hong Kong or Dubai.

Did your friend tell you about this fabulous chef, barely out of his teens, who made the best pasta they ever tasted? Would this be a great interview for a food or general magazine?

Did a colleague mention an expat who just bought a villa in Spain? Think property magazines or publications dedicated to Spain or expat communities.

How about this 60 year old woman helping out in a Kenyan school or the teenage girl down the road doing a parachute jump to raise funds for a children's hospital in Peru?

Have a look at possible markets, bearing in mind the topic should fit the readers' interests and age group. Your volunteer will be fine in a seniors' magazine but the teenager won't.

First things first

Which should you contact in the first instance, your subject or your magazine? Celebrities aside, I would say your subject. Tell them you would like to take photographs, they might want to have their hair done or wear their favorite shirt. As soon as you have secured content and pictures, you're ready to approach an editor. No one wants to disappoint an interviewee but if you let an editor down, that's worse for you.

However, should you plan to interview the Dalai Lama in time for Tibet Day, that's different. If it's topical, pitch straightaway or someone else will beat you to it.

Next comes research: the key to successful interviews. Find out as much as you can beforehand, regarding the topic and interviewee, particularly if they have a claim to fame. Don't ask a top chef in Rome where he learned his skills or when he took up his current position, look it up on his website. You will appear professional and save everybody's time.

Dress to suit. Jeans and sneakers will do if you're talking to a long distance hiker but won't go down well with the manager of a five star hotel.

Do

- Prepare your questions beforehand. Imagine you're a reader, what would you want to know, what would you ask?
- Start with easy questions to put your subject at ease.
- Maintain eye contact, take notes discreetly.
- Record the interview unless there are objections. This is for your own protection, in case of disagreement, and a back-up if doubts creep in. Did they say June or July? Get it right.
- Ask open questions, who, what, why, when, where, how.
- Listen.
- Be prepared to go off on a slant if an interesting fact comes to light. Your Lady Mayor for a woman's glossy takes her poodle to every meeting and he wears a mini-chain of honor. That's another feature for a dog magazine.
- Make a mental note of the environment, the cushions on a chair, the garden, the paintings on the wall, what the subject is wearing. Details will add color to your writing.
- Take photographs at the end: your subject will be more relaxed.
- Go through your notes when the interview is still clear in your mind.
- Send a thank you note the next day.

Don't

- Talk about yourself or interrupt, except to clarify a point.
- Let the interviewee distract you by asking questions about your own life.
- Guarantee publication unless you have a firm commission. If a magazine has expressed interest or you're a regular contributor, say it as it is.
- Offer payment, you are giving free publicity.

- Overstay your welcome.
- Let your subject read your piece prior to publication. You understand what the editor wants better than they do. If you're not sure about a fact, phone or email a specific question.

Take your Chance

Vietnam. Checked into my hotel late at night, heard a man talking about a lepers' village just over the pass. My train leaves at 8.00 in the morning. Plenty of time, booked a taxi for 5.00, hope it turns up.

When I get there, the manager doesn't speak a word of English but there's a nun who speaks French. I can cope with that. Amazing experience, one hour, two features, one for a Catholic newspaper (interview nun), the other a women's magazine (interview 26 year old girl caring for her sick parents). Possibly more.

Such encounters are a wonderful source of material for travel writers, opening our eyes to new situations and opportunities. You will find them all over the world, from craftsmen to Buddhist monks, from leg rowing fishermen in Burma to a local brass band. If possible, give your feature added value: don't interview any monk, try the eight year old, fresh from his village, or the trombone player approaching his 80th birthday.

Learn to eavesdrop, talk to strangers, with due care, make friends and you'll come across an exciting story. Chat to the unofficial guide outside the museum, the friendly receptionist, the taxi driver who's always there when you leave your hotel. Welcome their attention, show interest and sooner or later someone will take you where tourists don't go and maybe invite you into their home. They will give you your most original stories in return for a little business and perhaps one of those small presents you remembered to pack.

Now your turn

- Take a look at your local paper, it's full of people stories.
- Anyone suitable for interview, individual, association, for a regional magazine or a niche market?
- Give it a go, people love to talk about their hobbies, interests and even jobs.
- Remember to take pictures.

Top tips

1. It's all right to edit interviews to match the publication's style and word count, but do it within reason. Don't alter the meaning.
2. If you don't feel confident at first, practice with a friend before you try the real thing.

Done it? Great.

But don't put your camera away just yet...

Step 4

Photos Sell Stories

"Photography is pretty simple stuff. You just react to what you see."
Elliott Erwitt, photographer

Do you like snakes?

I don't but guess how I broke into travel writing? By posing with vipers (defanged) draped over my hands, shoulders, neck and head. I'd spotted a reader's holiday slot, wacky pictures essential, and in next to no time, I had both feet in the door of a top women's weekly.

Think Visuals

When you browse a magazine on the shelves, what do you look at first? Pictures, most likely. It's the same with editors and some will ask for photographs before commissioning, notably when you are new.

Why don't they use free images from CVBs and tourist boards? Some do but there's a lot of competition out there and most publications pride themselves on being original. Think about it: copy could be researched and written in-house but original pictures? Only a real traveler has them and this is where you come in. Today, most editors consider pictures part of the package, which means no extra pay, but it's a great way to impress.

Keep it simple

You don't have to be an expert unless you want to concentrate on photo essays. Learn the basics of digital photography (see *'Photography for Writers'* by Simon Whaley) and when you research your markets prior to a trip, consider what images they publish: humorous, dramatic, conventional, unusual, bright, atmospheric, people or landscapes.

For most magazine work, a compact camera will suffice as long as it takes high resolution images (eight million pixels upwards).The simpler the better, but I love an auto-intelligence mode which focuses clearly and corrects any shake. Read consumers' reviews, go for a reliable brand and a light model, for obvious reasons, and small, so it fits in your bag rather than dangle around your neck, drawing attention. Pack extra memory cards, battery, charger, adapter and a spare camera, in particular if you're venturing off the beaten track. A light tripod is useful.

Top tips

1. Take pictures of traveling companions and yourself on location, both portraits and action shots, to illustrate your feature or bio. Your current editor may not want them but perhaps others will at a later date.
2. Go for variety, for you never know what could come in handy, and caption as you go. One Chinese temple looks much like another but get it wrong and somebody will tell the editor. Credibility damaged.
3. How many pictures? The more, the better but consider the time it will take to sort them out.
4. Never forget how important your pictures are to give you a competitive edge and help you remember exactly how it was. Keep them safe on the road as you would cash or credit cards, and back them up as soon as possible.

Capture the Place

Did you notice the red dragon on a rooftop or the blue butterfly at your feet? Look up, look down, look behind you, but stop and take your time, your work and your life may depend on it if you happen to be teetering on the edge of a ravine. You'd also be wise to avoid army and police installations and personnel, airports in many countries and sometimes shots taken from the air. What about satellites, I asked? Well, that's different. Apart from that, it's all there for us but how do we start?

Act like a pro

Professionals get up at dawn when light and shadow add interest, contrast and perspective to any picture. Late afternoon is great too but it's best to avoid the midday glare unless a parade bursts out on the square or a royal helicopter lands on the school playing field. Try not to worry too much about the weather. Storm clouds add drama, drifting mist is atmospheric, white fluffy clouds in a blue sky are brilliant but when it's grey and dull, concentrate on interesting details while you wait for a better day.

Close ups are always useful: poppies, olives on a branch, food on a plate, a sari drying on a river bank, Berber silver in a souk, or architectural features, doorknobs, carved window frames, a circular seat around a tree.

As a photographer, you learn to adapt to circumstances, as explains Stuart Forster, photojournalist and travel writer, director of www.whyeyephotography.com.

When I'm on location I frequently have to be patient, for instance waiting for pedestrians to walk out of the frame around landmarks. Also, I might have to return to a scene to capture the ideal balance of light and shadow.

Yet at times I must react quickly. At the pilgrimage site of Fatima, I was photographing an open air mass when I noted a rare halo around the sun. I dropped to my knees to take pictures and to my surprise, the pilgrims thanked me for pointing out a new 'miracle of the sun'.

Top tips

1. Look at the postcards and shoot the usual angle for well-known places, some publications would like that, then seek a different view, get down on the grass, climb on a wall, see what it's like across the river.

2. Take several shots of a scene so you can offer originals to several markets. Photograph famous buildings when the place is quiet and again when crowds get there and add a sense of scale.

3. Framing is effective but don't overdo it. Classic frames include trees, flowers and archways but there's room for originality. I remember a winning image of the Taj Mahal taken across the river, framed by the horizontal line of a boat, the vertical silhouette of the punter and diagonal of his pole.

4. Scenery is often best if you lead the eye into the picture, maybe a path heading into the woods or a stile in the foreground adding depth to the landscape. Many publications welcome a sign of life in a landscape, a bicycle against a stone wall, a rucksack by the fence, sheep in a meadow.

5. Don't place the horizon in the center, move it up or down depending on conditions and the story you're trying to tell.

6. Most magazines love color. If a bleak landscape suits your theme, that's fine. Otherwise, add a touch of color, a scarf tied to a hiking pole, a ribbon caught on a fence, a sun hat, a book, anything that is relevant. Wear black by all means but always pack a little color and don't be afraid to use props, an umbrella, a picnic rug, anything that helps the story.

7. Catch the unusual, the monkey eating candyfloss, the rainbow over a castle, the sacred cow following a wedding party into the temple. Don't forget the occasional item

which will identify a place: a road sign, a London bus, a national flag.

8. Take pictures of funny signs, these can often be used on their own and bring extra cash. Recently spotted: 'free WiFi, pay toilets' (Kathmandu), 'I love you, darling, but please be gentle on my curves' (road bends in Himalaya).

Picture the People

People bring a place to life. Include them and readers will connect across the miles while editors will remember you for providing unique material. You weren't alone at Trooping the Color in London or the Lantern Festival in Taiwan but no one will have exactly the same pictures as you. Like the written word, images reveal your own view of the world and maybe something you spotted but no one else did.

Beware: if a sign says 'no photography', don't do it. Your images may be deleted or worse, you could be arrested. Note that in Islamic countries, photographing people is often a cultural taboo and that lives could be endangered if you publish pictures of refugees. But despite the inevitable restrictions, people are a gold mine for travel writers who tread thoughtfully.

Act sensibly
Should you hide in a corner and snap away or ask permission?

That depends how close you want to get and how you feel about it. Trust your intuition and if you are genuinely interested in the country and its people, you won't want to be a paparazzo. Groups are intimidating so it's better to approach on your own or maybe with a guide, engage in conversation, sign language works wonders, sit down, play with the children or help with homework and when everyone is smiling and relaxed, point to the camera and ask if it's ok. Most of the time, the answer is 'yes', especially if you lavish sufficient praise on that beautiful baby in her mother's arms.

There's only one problem: everyone stands to attention like soldiers on review. Fine, let's take a couple of pictures, relax, they'll do the same, then quick, catch them off guard and that's a winner.

Should you pay? That's up to you. Think how much the pictures are worth to you and what a few rupees would mean to your subject.

Should you tell them they may be published? In most cases, they'll be proud and excited, send them a copy.

What do editors really like?

- Bright colors, in most cases, especially red. Take a look at a few magazines and see for yourself.
- Pictures that tell a story: the boy collecting cow dung to plaster the walls, the bridegroom parading through the streets on a white horse, the child monk skipping down the path with an alms bowl on his head or the potter at the wheel. Get close and leave out the clutter, unless it's part of the story.
- Action: farmers planting rice, kids playing in the street, blacksmiths, woodcarvers, the stall holder tossing pancakes in the park.
- For groups of people, odd numbers as in flower arranging. Try it, it works, unless of course it's newly-weds or a mother and daughter story.

Any legal issues?
Possibly, notably in the West where the compensation culture has no bounds. Print your own model releases and carry them around: I (subject's name) give permission for photographs of myself and...., taken in... on (date), to be used for publication', signed by both of you and a third party if possible. Few people will decline but if they do, respect their wishes. Some publications insist on a model release both for locals and fellow travelers.

Public places aren't necessarily exempt. A girl sunbathing topless on a French beach may object to her picture in a magazine while someone supposedly away on business may not want to be seen hugging a glamorous blonde in Seville or Amsterdam.

Top tips

1. Enjoy the moment, savor the experience. Don't be so obsessed with pictures that you'll miss the dolphins popping out of the water or the paraglider rising in the currents. Otherwise, how will you write about it?
2. Always have your camera at hand. The best shots tend to turn up when you least expect them. Be prepared, whether you're on the road or in the air.
3. Close up or not, make sure the people in your photographs will appeal to your readers. In some cases, you may need to consider the way they dress, the age group and so on. Take a wide range to keep your options open, avoid smokers, unless you're making a point, and be aware that fashion can quickly date a picture.

Now your turn:
Buy two or three magazines and study the photographs:

- What are the popular subjects in each of the three?
- What colors, composition do they seem to favor?
- What differences do you notice between them?
- Which one do you prefer and why?

In the next few days, take pictures of people and places out of your comfort zone and at different times of day.

- When you get home, have a look at your images, what do you think?

- Which ones are best, why?
- Which ones didn't work out, why not?
- Consider how to improve and try again next week or next month. Better?

Now let's relax and see what it's like on the road.

A Day in the Life of a Travel Writer

5.30 am: Sunrise on the mountains, sheer magic, young woman performing a yoga 'salute to the sun', framed by the highest peak. Great picture for keep fit, yoga or soul and spirit.

7.30 am: Breakfast in the lodge then three hour walk down to the valley. Tempted to take a short cut through the woods but pictures much better along the road, villages, farmers, local life. Stopped to chat to weavers.

11.30 am: Reached main road, taxi to the monastery. Looked around temples and shrines then a monk came along to show me 'what the tourists don't see'. Great photos, well worth a donation.

4.00 pm: Returned to the lake, grabbed a pancake. My usual guide was waiting, boat to the island with evening pilgrims. Dozens of boats, one had a leak and everyone had to get out and paddle, women carrying children, saris dripping wet. Action shots.

5.30 pm: Back to hotel, appointment with manager for tour, took a few pictures, shower and diary.

6.30 pm: Interview chef and dinner at the Paradise. Joined by middle-aged man who turned out to be a poet, indulged in flamboyant serenade for 30 minutes, loved posing for the camera. Definitely a piece for a writers' magazine. Wife arrived, had a chat about the plight of local women. Useful, learned a lot.

9.00 pm: Traditional dancing, join in and take pictures.

11.00 pm: Back in my room. Hotel will arrange bicycle for the morning, 8.30, what a treat. Caption images, complete notes, final check on tomorrow's itinerary.

Now you understand: it's exciting, amazing, often frantic, but no one will mind if you take a break occasionally. Time out, 30 minutes? Go online, share the day's adventure with like-minded people and keep on writing while you're on the road.

Enjoy...

Step 5

Get Online

"Blogging is a great way to show your talents and interests to prospective employers."
Lauren Conrad, designer and author

Today, no writer can ignore the web. Creative space, marketing tool, potential money spinner, what more could you ask for? Write as you travel, record your adventure when it's fresh in your mind, upload your images and keep in touch with followers and friends. Back home, it will provide exciting material and complement your diary. Read it, tailor it and you will be ready for the next step.

Blog as you Go
Do you have a blog? This is what it could do for you:

- You write whatever you wish, whenever you like and in any way you want. If you enjoy writing in the first person, that's perfect, a blog is about sharing your experience and expressing your personality.
- You don't have to wait for assignments and publication is guaranteed.
- Your work will be read around the world. Elephants in Thailand? Cycling in Tuscany? An editor could be looking to commission your topic.
- As well as your words, you showcase your pictures. The more exposure you gain, the better.
- It's an extra link on your business card, or when you pitch to print editors, and a chance to keep writing when work is scarce.

Blogging won't make you rich overnight, or pay for your next vacation, but if you persevere, you might get there in the end. In the early days however, think of it as a platform rather than a wage earner and a chance to practice your writing skills.

Your choice
Set up a free blog on a hosting site such as wordpress.com or blogspot.com, an easy task but limited by a set format, or be a guest on existing travel blogs.

If you can afford it however, claim a domain name and self-host your blog. This gives you more flexibility in the design and allows the URL to stand on its own, giving your work professional status among millions of casual bloggers. It can double up as your personal website. Choose a name that highlights your interests and attracts the right readers. If you're after page views and cash, self-hosting is the best option (available on wordpress.com).

Numbers matter
Either way, numbers dictate revenue: the more page views you get, the more advertising you attract, for yourself or your host.

How do you increase page views?

- Update and post at least once a week.
- Understand and interact with your readers, take note of their comments.
- Maintain quality and interest.
- Specialize if you can, food, Africa, luxury travel.
- Be active on social media, build up a following and post links.
- Don't be gimmicky but make your site attractive and include lots of images.

Experienced blogger Kathryn Burrington tells us how visuals make a difference:

Coming from a graphic design and photography background has been a great advantage for me. People often jump around the net from one site to another and there are so many blogs out there. You need to make yours stand out and grab people's attention visually. Otherwise many visitors won't hang around long enough to start reading. Quality photography is important and every blogger should invest in Photoshop Elements. Even just using the auto smart fix can work wonders on your photos. www.travelwithkat.com

Could you be an Expert?

If you have sufficient expertise in a particular field, a destination, an age group, an activity, rail travel, luxury spas in Asia, you might consider setting up a specialist website. It isn't essential to know everything before you begin but be prepared to fill in the gaps and update frequently. These sites are third person and information-based but can accommodate personal features as well.

To monetise your efforts, your theme must attract a wide enough audience but be tightly focused. The URL should stand out among those of tour operators and CVBs or tourist boards. Take a look for example at www.activecaribbean.com covering 37 destinations, reporting not on beaches but activity holidays, hiking, golf, cooking and more. The Caribbean attracts close to 25 million visitors every year. Compare with Bhutan, barely 70,000 maximum page views? You understand what I mean.

Setting up a website involves a lot of work, time and expense if you hire a professional designer but there are cheaper options. Look up www.sitesell.com or 'best web hosting sites'. Some offer a refund if you are not satisfied.

Fine Tuning

Blogging allows you to express yourself and share your travels. On the other hand, information sites are mostly about facts, a place where readers come looking for answers. In this case, the style is straightforward rather than literary and there are important points to remember.

- Titles: ask yourself what a reader interested in your topic would type into a search engine, Malaysia Golf , Food in Sicily, London Luxury Hotel Hyde Park. That's your title, anything fancy and readers won't find you.
- The web is for surfing, attention span is short. Forget your 2000 words, 500 will keep your visitor reading to the end of the page. If you plan 2000 words to do justice to your topic, consider splitting it into four posts and you could quadruple your page views.
- Familiarize yourself with search engine optimization (SEO). This means using keywords relevant to your page that will attract interested viewers and in due course, advertisers. Have one or two in your title (as above), sprinkle others in your text but don't overdo it. Search engines treat keyword stuffing as spam, sending you shooting down from page 3 to page 47. No one gets that far.
- Entertain your readers by all means but if you want them to come back, give them what they're looking for at the same time. Let a blog speak about a place, not just about you.

Top tip
Writing for the web is fun, brilliant for self-promotion and can be surprisingly lucrative in the long run but don't use it as an excuse to neglect print. If you are starting and want a quick gain, that's where the money is and where your writing will truly impress.

Remember what they said about cinemas when video tapes appeared? Yet, we still go to the movies. Print will be with us for a long time yet.

Are you ready for it?

Winning Ideas

"Everything begins with an idea."
Earl Nightingale, speaker and author

Editors are busy people with readers to please, pages to fill and deadlines to meet.

What do they want?

Great ideas, great pictures.

What don't they want?

Your holiday story from beginning to end unless it was exceptional.

A request for ideas.

What their staff could write at no extra cost.

'I've just been to Japan and hope you will be interested in an article about my trip. I went to Tokyo, Kyoto.....What would you like me to write about?'

You'll be lucky to get a reply.

As a freelance writer, your job is to offer suitable ideas to editors, not the other way round. True, there is scope in some markets for edited versions of your holiday but to get the upper hand, go for a fresh tightly-focused angle. Every destination is filled with wonders and each one is a potential article. Don't try to cover it all in 1000 words.

This is the advice of Ashley Gibbins, Chief Executive of the International Travel Writers Alliance:

Travel writers today should focus on the 'little picture' that will hook readers and editors. A web address will always provide the 'big picture'.

A feature on Naples, Italy, will be far more interesting if it's the tale of a three generation family working on a fishing boat than one which takes the old route of when to go, what to do and where to stay. And the resulting images will be far more enticing.

What's your Type?

What sort of features do you like to read?

Flick through a range of magazines and you'll notice that travel articles fall broadly into five categories.

Browse the following samples and tick your preference(s):

- Destination piece, usually a lengthy feature assigned to an expert or established writer and possibly the most difficult to sell for a freelance, unless the destination is unusual. It shows what a place is like, how it feels, what you might want to do and see. It's objective and factual but must paint a scene to entice readers:

Some say St George's is the prettiest capital in the Caribbean, all pastel-colored roofs tumbling down to the harbor framed by lush volcanic cones. It's small enough to explore on foot and guarded by an eighteenth century fort on a rocky headland. Up there the wind howls on the battlements but you soon forget the climb as you gaze at the southern cliffs, the cruise terminal, the lagoon speckled with sails and the glistening crescent of the inner harbor.

- Practical advice, lists (top theme parks, best beaches), travel tips (for families, seniors, saving money), reviews, what to do in 24 or 48 hours.

Home vacation for the Brits:

Are you looking for somewhere different, ideal for children, but you don't want to travel far? Try the Isle of Man in the Irish Sea. The island has more to offer than you could pack in a week and every attraction brings its unique brand of Manx spirit.

Here are 10 reasons to take the family across the water.

- Personal experience: a festival, a visit to a wild life sanctuary, a dramatic or humorous event or a journey:

"Chiya, Didi? You like tea?"

Som, my Nepalese guide of many years, knows me well. The lodge is cosy and warm, flasks glow like rainbows on the shelves, salted tea, butter tea, milk tea, lemon tea. I settle for the latter under the glare of the resident goat. Blackened pots bubble in the hearth, chicken heads and scraps of buffalo meat hang from the rafters.

"Only five days walk to my native village,' says Som, 'and we will meet my older sister."

- Special interest, food, cultural tours, activity vacations, nature, conservation, history, anniversaries:

Our flamboyant tutor swept in like a ray of sunshine.

'We'll start with observational drawing,' she announced, as she arranged potted plants on the desk. Geraniums, petunias, perfect match for her dress. 'Don't worry, you can't make a mistake, it's all about personal interpretation.'

At the French House Party, the time had come to get down to business. No more lounging by the pool or sipping wine in the shade as we had done on arrival, at least not until the afternoon. For us budding artists, that was the great attraction, work in the morning, lunch al fresco then chill out for the rest of day.

- People stories: reports or interviews of artisans, artists, local celebrities, business people, anyone who has something to say or show out of the ordinary:

Adele's story begins like a fairytale.

"I woke up one morning and remembered a dream, so vivid, so real, I knew instantly it would change my life. There I was, running my own restaurant in London. Why? How? I didn't know. I had studied languages at University, I was working in the City, perhaps I was just ready for change."

Bright eyes, big smile and silky blonde hair, Adele was born in Britain but looks fresh from Italy and whenever she visits her relatives, she feels at home. On that special day in 2010, she decided to follow her dream.

Did you tick every type? That's fine, they overlap. The location is always there, central to the piece or secondary to the theme.

Now your turn
Think back to your last trip, or consider your neighborhood, and jot down ideas.

- Destination? Home or vacation, think of a village, a city or a specific area you could write about, large or small.
- Advice? Read your notes, or walk around the streets, what could you group in a round-up, what tips would you offer to would-be visitors, is there a hotel, a spa or restaurant worthy of a review?
- Personal experience? If it's home, what makes it special for you? Maybe you'd like to take the reader down memory lane, a 'then and now' piece? Or imagine you're a visitor: what would be interesting in the neighborhood? If it's a vacation, which particular place, activity or journey sticks in your mind?

- Special interest? Did you camp in the jungle, go on a sailing course, visit gardens in Malta? At home, what are your hobbies, food, dance, hiking or playing chess?
- People? If you didn't interview on your last vacation, remember to do it next time. At home, talk to your friends, ask around, contact a local club and identify the most interesting character.

Writing about home isn't exotic but it's full of opportunities. Dig them out, do your research and welcome the chance to hone your skills while you wait for the next big trip.

Plenty of ideas?

Well done, that's the first leap on the road to publication.

Let it Flow

"The way to get good ideas is to get lots of them and throw away the bad ones."
Linus Pauling, scientist

So let's zoom in on your favorite ideas or destination and all the relevant material you gathered through research and on location. Brilliant, but how will you identify the gems that will make your copy sparkle?

This is what works for me: setting time aside to sift through diary and other material, on long haul return flight or as soon as possible at home, then sorting out material on spread sheet or paper, in sections with brief references.

Take Bangkok for example:

Section 1:   Temples

Temple of Dawn , D10, G35 (diary p:10, guide book p:35)

Reclining Buddha, D26, G58, V6 (visitors' guide)

Marble Temple, D4, G9

Emerald Buddha, D2, 46, 62, G20

Section 2: Waterways

Traveling on the river, water buses/taxis, long boats, D3, 15, 56, G69

Waterside attractions, D39, G46, also temple section plus palace

Trip on the canals D25, G48, V10

Floating market, refer to market section

Day trip to Ayutthaya, river cruise, D32 plus website

Section 3: Food

Street stalls...

Markets...

Dining with Thai family

Seafood restaurants

Best rooftop bars

Section 4: Shopping

Affordable, luxury, best buys, crafts...

Section 5: Entertainment

Patpong hot spots, classical dance, other

Section 6: Day trips from Bangkok

Rose Garden, Floating Market, Ayutthaya

Add accommodation, parks, heritage buildings, museums, local transport and anything else you came across and the whole experience is right there in front of you, neatly packaged with easy references. You can pull out anything you want in minutes, now and in the future.

Now your turn

What was your favorite idea?

Is all your material at hand?

Sift through and organize, it might take time but you'll only need to do it once.

Less is More

Now that you have identified the bare bones of your trip, what do you do with them?

Let's return to Bangkok:

> You could cash in on the current trend and go for a round up, top three places to buy gold in Bangkok, best vegetarian restaurants near city center, top ten nightclubs in Patpong, or suggest what to do on a stopover. Or concentrate on one section, temples, waterways, better still narrow it down to a single nugget, Emerald Buddha, Floating Market.

Research, find your voice, follow your passion.

Did you visit the Louvre museum in Paris? Could you write about one specific exhibition that inspired you? Did you have a vacation on a hotel barge in the south of France? Was the food outstanding? Call it a gourmet cruise and make gastronomy your center piece.

Been to London?

Sights, things to do, museums, festivals, food, great topics but too big.

How about the following?

- Food: Best places for afternoon tea in Central London
- Festivals: New Year in China Town
- Westminster Abbey: Behind the scenes
- Things to do: Free attractions for families, ten of the best
- Sightseeing: Bus tour on the ghost trail
- Quirky wedding venues in the capital

The tighter the focus, the more original you are likely to be, the more features you can write and the more you'll earn, whether it's about home or an exotic vacation.

Now your turn

- Think of a city, either where you live, or recently visited, and see if you can come up with three ideas. Or perhaps you're planning to go somewhere soon? Research and do likewise.
- Or have you just had a great adventure?

Let me share this one from a student raving about her African safari. Nothing unusual though, who would publish it? Then she told us about watching the birth of a zebra and its death, 30 minutes later, in a lion's jaws. Now, her experience was unique and tightly focused. She called it '30 minutes from birth to death' and within two days, the story was sold.

Did you notice the word 'story'?

That's because an article isn't only about facts, it's about a story, your story, what you did, saw, experienced, even when you're writing in the third person. That's what appeals to editors, what the staff sitting at their desk cannot offer.

- Do you have a special story? If you think hard enough, you may well find one and that will be a winning idea.

Find the Angle

Editors always welcome topical items, a new museum, a wine tour off the beaten track, a boutique hotel opening up in a light-house or a journey in the footsteps of a famous traveler, 100 years on. Has a celebrity just bought a property in your area or was the latest box office hit filmed down the road? Just make sure you're first to pitch.

Likewise, festivals tend to do well, cutting reeds for the Queen in Swaziland, flying kites in Indonesia, shooting poisoned arrows through the canopy in Malaysia. Pitch before you go or save your material and try early next time.

An article aims to entertain readers, with just enough facts to answer their questions. If you want your copy to shine, ask yourself what made your trip different from others, what would spur an editor to read beyond the opening line.

Consider the following questions and you may come up with a winning angle:

- Why did you go to India, New Zealand or Spain?

  Were you celebrating a birthday or anniversary, meeting a penfriend, researching a family tree, attending a wedding, revisiting childhood haunts, learning a skill, pursuing a hobby? The reason could be your theme, the canvas on which you embroider the destination as you wish.

- Who traveled with you?

  If you went solo, what were the pros and cons? Can you share your experience with others considering a similar trip?

  If you traveled with friends, what was it like? A colleague of mine sailed the Norfolk Broads, nothing new, but she titled her piece 'Three women in a boat', brilliant angle.

  Did you travel with your daughter, father, long lost uncle, a complete stranger? Your companions could give your story that little extra.

  Did you have teenagers in tow? What was it like for you and for them?

- How did you travel?

  Boat, cycle, gypsy caravan, hire car, horseback, on foot, train, truck, rickshaw, motorbike...

  What were the highlights, the amusing or scary parts of the trip? A journey alone can fill 1000 words.

- What did you do that was special?

  Did you learn calligraphy in a Buddhist monastery?

  Did you trek with a donkey or go skiing in summer?

  Did you eat in the world's largest communal kitchen?

- Who did you meet?
  A five minute encounter could produce 500 words. Mine was a holy man who did amazing feats with his private parts, on his own, I'm glad to say. My guide averted his eyes but I watched eagerly and had no problem selling the piece.

Now your turn

- Go back to your top idea and answer the questions outlined above: why, who, how, what.
- Anything that could give you a unique angle, a tight focus?
- Look at your pictures, would they fit?

Top tips

1. Beware of overworked themes, such as 'the other side of,' it may be new to you but it's probably been done.
2. If you have a winning idea but can't get images, tell the editor straightaway. If they're hot on the story, they will source the pictures.
3. Seek the difference but always keep your readers in mind. Ever been stalked by a tiger? Now, who would want to read about that?
4. If anything disrupts your plans, consider it an opportunity. A landslide, a cancelled flight, nowhere to sleep for the night, worth 300 words? You bet.
5. Don't be tempted to fantasize. Some readers will act on what you say and if you must warn them, try a touch of humor or a positive slant. Compare 'don't drink tap water, it isn't safe' to 'drink only bottled water, it's widely available and cheap.'

Nearly there...

Step 7

Getting it Right

"It's the little details that are vital. Little things make big things happen."
John Wooden, coach

Spot the Difference
Well done, you have brilliant ideas and can't wait to get started.

Thank you for staying with me so far but it isn't time to write just yet. Before you type a single word, it's important to identify the right publication.

Below are two excerpts from published articles.

How many differences can you spot? The more the better.

Think about the angle, the likely readership, the tone of voice and choice of vocabulary.

(Answers at the end of this chapter)

1. Ben Nevis, Scotland
Three generations to the top

"What is the best day to go to the top?"
"Thursday, 30% cloud."
The challenge was on, three generations to the top of Ben Nevis, grandson Sidney, aged 13, daughter Stella and myself, on the wiser side of middle age. We rose bright and early, packed a map, a whistle and lots of energy food. Sidney was happy.

Glancing at the trail I felt fully reassured. With scores of people stepping up into the sunshine, from pole-swinging mountaineers to mums and dads with toddlers in tow, it couldn't be that hard. Black-faced sheep munched in the meadows and the path crawled up the mountainside in long leisurely zigzags and the occasional steps.

"Did they really plan to bring a train up here?" asked Sidney.

The Victorians were full of ideas, summit hotel, observatory, pony track, but the railway remained a dream. The Ben was spared although over the years it saw many a strange thing struggling up its slopes, a wheelbarrow, a horse-drawn cart, a piano and the Ben Runners who have myriad stories to tell, from a romantic marriage proposal to dancing the Highland Fling on the top.

But running wasn't for us... We plodded on, reveling in the fresh mountain air, looking out for blueberries, heather and great swathes of luminous fern which left their scent in the air. Lizards basked on the stones, wheatears and meadow pipits burst into song...

2. Cyprus
Island of love

Imagine a beautiful island of sandy beaches and pine-covered hills, glorious sunsets and to spice it all up, the very place where Aphrodite, the Greek Goddess of Love, rose from the waves. Wherever you go in Cyprus, you're sure to follow in her footsteps. There's her bathing pool, temple, beach and the spring where according to legend, a quick swig is enough to arouse the most delicious passion.

And that's not all the magic on this island which has bewitched the likes of Leonardo DiCaprio and Posh and Becks. From the sweeping bays of the west to Agia Napa in the east, beaches lure you with tingling sands and crystal clear waters. If you fancy plenty of buzz and a bit of exploring, Limassol is your best bet...

No one will mind if you hug the beach from morning to

night but to see the real Cyprus, you'll have to head into the mountains where white villages nestle among vineyards and orange groves... Be prepared for dizzying heights but when you gaze at the Rock of Aphrodite glowing all coppery gold far below, you may well feel a flutter down your spine. They say the local hunks swim naked around it to catch sight of the goddess so if you're in the mood for love, that's definitely the place to be.

Fact box: shopping, nightlife, food

Which excerpt did you prefer and why?

No doubt one will appeal more than the other and in the early days, it's good to concentrate on markets where you feel at ease. But when you are ready, if you want to make your writing pay, you will be able to tackle all manners of ideas and adapt your style to various outlets. It's a challenge but when you succeed, you'll be amazed.

Match to Market

Should you start at the top in search of the best rates or at the lower end where competition is less? It really depends how you feel, how original your idea is and how great your pictures are. Either way, draw up a list of possibilities and if your first market doesn't work, move on to the next. Being proactive will keep you in a positive mood.

Go back to your original market research then take a fresh look on the shelves. Maybe new titles have emerged, others have gone without trace or a new editor brought in change. If a publication states 'no freelance', forget it, but 'no unsolicited contributions' simply means you must pitch first and even if most contributors appear on the staff list, it's worth a try. No editor wants to miss out on a great scoop.

Know your readers

As in any other business, the product has to fulfil the clients' needs. Would you sell a lawnmower to a resident on the 10th floor of an apartment block or a racing car to a man on the minimum wage?

Editors are our front line, they understand their readers to a tee and whatever they publish is designed to meet their expectations. Their job depends on it. Luckily for us, they have done most of the research.

This is what to look for:

- Age group
- Status: single, relationship, married, parents, grandparents
- Interests, lifestyle
- Education
- Culture
- Income, jobs

This is how you can tell:

- Look at the photographs: they show the age, sex and status of readers, their lifestyle and interests, especially on the cover though this is often exaggerated to draw attention.
- Check the adverts: no advertisers will waste their budget on the wrong clientele. Anti-wrinkle cream indicates middle-aged females, stair lifts over 60s, diapers young families.
  Adverts also relate to the lifestyle and likely budget. Is it about a US$5000 cruise or backpacking in Nepal? A day in a luxury spa or aromatherapy at home? Gold pendants or a karaoke set?
- Read the letters and editor's page, consider the free offers and competitions and you'll know what appeals to the readership.

- Notice the price of the publication and quality of print and paper, this tends to reflect the buyers' budget.

Study every page to build a complete picture then concentrate on the travel section, both adverts and content. Are the readers armchair travelers or real adventurers? Is it about short or long haul destinations, run of the mill or off the beaten track vacations? What type of accommodation do they feature? What kind of interests: nightlife, shopping, sports, cultural tours?

Now your turn
Go back to your top idea and decide who might be interested, family, single, senior, and which magazine they might buy. That's your number one market.

Keep going until you have three or more possibilities but don't rely on a single issue. Study at least two recent copies.

Think beyond the obvious.
Did you go on a painting vacation in Corfu? You may consider an art magazine but unless you had a celebrity tutor or learned an innovative technique, chances are it's been done. How about a general publication or one specialising in Greece or active seniors?

Look for slots beyond the main travel page, maybe hotel of the week or room with a view, letters inviting replies or readers' contributions such as it happened to me or my holiday from hell. Handle the latter with care for you could put people's jobs at risk or end up in court.

Consider all sorts of markets and multiple sales.

Travel writer Mari Nicholson gives us two examples:

I had two commissions upfront when I went to Bali then I witnessed a tooth filing. It was the groom's present to his bride, her teeth filed in public by an old man wielding a large metal file while tears poured down her cheeks. It made me think. I approached *Dental Hygiene and The International Dental Conference Magazine*. They loved it. Always go for the odd angle.

New Year's Eve on Copacabana Beach in Rio: priestesses casting spells, visitors falling into trances and the throb of the samba drums escalating the excitement. Too good to keep to myself, I thought, so I told the world about it, three magazines, one newspaper and a Radio Broadcast.

Learn to think out of the box.

Who would take an article on Chinese embroidery? Not a single reply from the obvious needlework markets. I had almost brushed it aside when a competition turned up: lateral thinking, 500 words, specific angle but should target unexpected market.

What was the most popular topic for the embroidery? Cats, so there it was, Chinese embroidery for a cat magazine.

First prize then sold to Your Cat.

Always look out for competitions. Even the short list is a huge confidence boost and if the work is published, it could be the start of your portfolio.

Now your turn

Cut a sheet of paper into 12 pieces, six on one side, each one with the name of a magazine, six on the other, each one with an idea.

Fold them up, pick one from each pile. Can you think of a link?

Try it from time to time and surprise yourself. Let your imagination roam and if one match is going to work, it's worth it.

Top tips

1. Be flexible: if you are the same age as your readers and share their interests, it will be easier to write for them but

it isn't essential. As long as you understand their mind set, you can do it.

2. If you're thinking global markets, be aware of cultural differences and politics. Here are three examples:

   Avoid lists of 4 or its multiples in Asian publications, the number (similar to the word death) is often considered unlucky.

   Don't write about wine in a dry country or pork in Islamic cultures.

   Tread carefully with Tibet or Taiwan in Chinese publications, in case you need a visa in the future.

Perfect Pitch

You have a great idea, you have identified the perfect market, plus a few in reserve, can you start writing?

No, I would definitely recommend pitching in the first instance.

Why it's best to pitch first

- It saves time for editors: a pitch is quick to read but 1800 words landing in an inbox from an unknown sender, at the end of a busy day? Remember how easy it is to delete.

- It saves time for writers: you might search the archives to see what has been featured in the past year, but how do you know what is scheduled next week or in two or six months' time?

- It's better for your morale: spending three days on an article and having it returned is discouraging, an hour or even half a day preparing a query letter isn't so bad.

- Pitch first and you could sell every article you write. That makes you a professional, always working on assignment and making the most efficient use of your writing time.

Brief and brilliant

- Give yourself plenty of time to craft your query. It might take a whole morning but your success depends on it.
- Send by email but only when you feel it's absolutely right. You can't change your mind once you've clicked 'send'.
- Address it to the correct editor, that's the travel editor; if there isn't one, the features editor or for a niche publication, the editor. If details are not in the current issue, phone the switchboard and make sure you have the correct spelling, is it Ann or Anne? If you can't get this right, why should they trust you?
- Use the appropriate term of address. 'Hi John' will do for a backpackers' magazine but 'Dear...' is better for seniors. Is there an editorial letter on the first page? How does the editor address the readers? A suitable greeting shows editors you are familiar with their publication.
- Take great care over the subject line: 'Have you ever slept with a buffalo?' I once wrote. Good intro for a feature, I thought, but I never had the chance. As a subject, it looked like spam. Go for clarity and be specific, mentioning destination plus angle: 'Sumatra, longhouse trek' or 'Crete for families, West is best'.
- Show the editor you have read the magazine by pitching in a similar style, consider the tone and vocabulary.
- Get straight to the point, don't waste space or time talking about your wonderful holiday. This is about your idea, not your life.
- Keep it short. If you cannot sum up your subject in a couple of paragraphs, how can you write a whole feature within the word count?
- Don't reveal everything in your letter, just enough to whet the editor's appetite.
- Mention images, anything topical and add your website or

relevant organizations to your contact details.

Example 1

Sometimes, notably in human interest stories, the first paragraph of your feature makes a good pitch:

> Babu is four, maybe five. He sits on the edge of the Durbar Square, shuffling from time to time to follow the shade. He has no pants, no shoes, his only possession is a plastic bag to wrap around his feet at night. No one knows where he comes from, he's one of 1000 children living on the streets in Kathmandu.
>
> Picture enclosed.
>
> Would you like to read more?

The answer came within 30 minutes, please send it straightaway.

I pleaded for an extra 12 hours, not quite ready, I said, and stayed up half the night.

The magazine used it for their Christmas appeal.

Example 2

Here's another query also on Nepal but this one for a Soul and Spirit publication.

> They say Pokhara is the most beautiful valley on earth with the snowy peaks of Annapurna mirrored in the placid waters of Fewa Lake. Every day, from dawn to dusk, pilgrims laden with offerings make their way to the island. There are no motor boats, only paddles and oars.
>
> It's the perfect place to reflect and connect with your inner self and the natural world, the abode of spirits and gods, at its most stunning.
>
> What do you think?

What to leave out

- Your CV and any negative remarks about yourself, such as 'I have never been published'. What counts is your idea, not your records, unless you are asked for them.
- Money talk, wait until you have secured an assignment.
- Request for guidelines. They will be on the website or the editor expects potential contributors to buy the magazine and draw their own conclusions. If you can't do that, forget it.
- Attachments: whether it's examples of work or large photo files unless requested. Some editorial desks treat attachments from unknown senders as spam.

Top tips

1. Don't phone editors unless you have burning news or they've told you it's ok. They may be up against a deadline or just back from a meeting which didn't go well. Emails can wait, phone calls don't. No one likes interruptions.
2. Choose a sensible time to send your query, 5.00 p.m. on Friday or first thing on Monday aren't the best. I tend to go for mid-week.
   If you know when an issue is due to the printer's, avoid the run up to the deadline. Wait until the pressure is off.
3. For seasonal features, approach editors well ahead of the time. Some monthlies plan their schedule up 12 months in advance.
4. When the editor gives you the go ahead, don't change your mind or make excuses. Get on with it or you'll lose credibility. There's always a way to fulfil the brief, even if it means an unexpected trip, extra research or sourcing images.
5. An expression of interest isn't a commission. It means 'send us the finished piece and if we like it, we'll buy it.' It

is however a positive reply and it's up to you to get it right.

6. If your pitch doesn't make it, take it in your stride. You are not being rejected, neither is your idea. If you did your homework, you got it right. Most likely, the editor has a similar piece in the pipeline or enough material for the next six months.

7. It's fine to pitch to non-competing markets at the same time, providing you can deliver. Each one should be offered a different angle and pictures.

Now your turn
Consider your idea:

Can you sum it up in five words or less? Great, this is your subject line.

Take another look at your potential readers. Would this appeal to them and the editor? Perfect.

Ready to pitch? A couple of paragraphs should do it but make them brilliant, this is your only sales tool.

Good luck…

Make it Fit

Wow, it's a 'yes', great idea, perfect outlet and positive response, superb. Get it right and you will sell.

Your challenge is simple:

Be yourself but write for your readers.

Editors know best
Which magazine do you buy on a regular basis? Why do you like it?

Perhaps it's a quick read, no article longer than 800 words, chatty style and colorful pictures?

How would you feel if you were suddenly faced with 2000 word articles, a stern academic tone and a mere sprinkling of images?

If it was me, I'd be shocked and look elsewhere.

Most of us pick up a magazine because we like the look of it, the content and images, just as they are, and if we subscribe or purchase on a regular basis, it's like being part of a club. It's familiar, reassuring, something to look forward to every week or every month. Don't you agree?

Editors understand that. They spend a lot of time assessing the readership and any change they bring is likely to be the result of a survey or an outburst of disgruntled letters. That's why, even if the editor loves your idea, you can't write the copy any way you want. I started that way but realized a 10% chance of success wasn't worth the hard work. I learned the most important lesson: writing comes at the end, not the beginning. Today, I cannot write a single word until I have decided which market I am targeting.

So here's the final hurdle:

Take another close look at your chosen market. This time, it's serious: if you get every detail right in your copy, you will save the editor time and show you are aware of the magazine's ethos. That will earn you a place in everyone's good books and your name will be passed around as a reliable travel writer.

Worth the effort?

Sure, but do it every single time for you are only as good as your last piece.

Now let's concentrate on your model travel page and study the format, house style and tone.

Format

- Count the words: no guess work please. Don't stray any further than 20 words either way. Too long means editorial time will be needed to cut, too short and there will be a gap on the page.

- Check paragraphs: how many are there, how many lines on average, are they indented or not, should you leave a line between them?
- Breaking up the copy: are there any subtitles, how many, or is it an extra blank line between sections? Or one big chunk of writing?
- Check sentences: do they tend to be short or run to several lines, or both?
- Check words: are there any long words or are they mostly 2-3 syllables, any foreign words?
- Is there a fact box? What information does it contain: where to stay, eat, getting there, any comments? Is a phone number preceded by 'phone' or 'tel.'? In which order do contacts appear, email or website first? How many words does the box contain? If a box is required, you must provide it but place it at the end of the copy, clearly marked 'fact box' or 'more info' as labeled in the magazine.

House style

- Is it English or US spellings?
- English or US grammar?
- Weights and measures: imperial or metric?
- Currency: is it euros, sterling, dollars, abbreviated or not?
- Time: 12 or 24 hour clock?
- Numbers, are they in figures or letters? The usual rule is letters up to ten but there are exceptions.
- Contractions: should you use 'it's' or 'it is', 'can't' or 'cannot', 'st' or 'saint', 'doesn't' or 'does not'?
- Abbreviations: are there any? How are they explained?

Tone

- Does the writer use first person, 'I' or 'we', or is it third person? If it's 'we', make sure readers understand who you are. If it's 'I', use it sparingly, with a few facts or descriptions in between. It doesn't do to push yourself to the front on every other line.
- Does the writer address the reader? 'If you go there', 'you might prefer to take the kids to...'
- Is the tone formal or chatty, do the words lean towards the Queen's English or everyday slang?
- Would readers speak about their partner, husband or hubby? Their children or their kids? Their friend or their mate? Would they say 'my mother and I' or 'me and my Mom'? The magazine mirrors its readers, the answer is on the page.
- Are there snippets of dialogues?
- Questions to draw the reader in, such as 'did you know', 'have you ever been'?
- Do local characters or other travelers appear in the story? Any quotes?
- Any anecdotes or is it more about facts?
- Is atmosphere important?
- Humor welcome?
- Is the present tense acceptable to bring your trip to life? Some editors love it, others hate it.

Answers to 'spot the difference':

1. Ben Nevis

Published in People's Friend, a traditional weekly magazine with strong family values, keen on nostalgia and the countryside, aimed mostly at middle-aged women and beyond.

The three generation theme would appeal, as would Ben

Nevis; the magazine is based in Scotland.

Notice:

- Use of the first person
- Snippets of dialogue
- Everyday vocabulary but no slang
- Mentions of plants, lizards, birds
- Touches of humor
- Reference to Victorians
- Anecdotes
- Sight, sound and smell

2. Cyprus

Published in Reveal, aimed at young women, single or in a relationship but no children, looking for romance, beach holidays, nightlife, shopping, interested in celebrities.

Notice:

- Use of 'you' instead of first person, addressing readers
- Casual vocabulary, swig, local hunks, plenty of buzz
- Grammar reflecting the spoken word, there's her bathing pool, temple... 'And' starting a new paragraph.
- Romantic words, with a touch of exaggeration, magic, bewitched, delicious passion, hug the beach
- Platitudes: glorious, beautiful
- Reference to celebrities
- Hint of the island's other attractions
- Fact box attuned to readers' interests

Did you spot any more?

Add them to the list.

All Set, Ideas, Markets?
Let's Go...

Step 8

Time to Write

"The secret of becoming a writer is to write... and keep on writing."
Ken MacLeod, writer

Excellent, now you have:

- the right destination
- the right angle
- the right market
- the right images and you have secured interest from an editor.

All in the Mind

But what's happening?

Starting, stopping, can't do it...

Are you suffering from writer's block?

I have good news:

Writer's block does not exist, it's all in the mind, a lack of confidence or an excuse to be idle so all you have to do is change your mind set.

Facts, anecdotes, you have it all, what's stopping you?

Adopt a 'can do' attitude, decide what you will write and when, then get on with it. You owe it to yourself. Make it a habit and rewards will be greater than you ever imagined.

Here are three easy steps to help you start:

1. Map it out

Decide what you want to 'visit' along the way and plan the best route, for instance:

Destination: Tenerife

Angle: family attractions
Market: holiday magazine (self-catering)
Word count: 1000
What to include? beaches, theme parks, boat trips (watching whales and dolphins), soft adventure (volcano by cable car).

Four sections, 220-250 words each, allowing for beginning and end, flexibility allowed.

The route? Start with whales and dolphins (action scene), then beaches and related activities, followed by inland adventure (would the kids like a change?) and ending with a bang, theme parks/family fun.

2. Warm up
Cold starts don't work for cars or for me. Many of my students feel the same. Give us a sheet of paper, a theme, 100 words to write in 15 minutes, and more often than not, the page is blank or leads nowhere. Your mind is your friend, give it time to think, mull over your ideas and when it is ready, it will let you know.

Do your thinking when you're cooking, cleaning the car or cycling home from work and you will realize that physical activity increases blood flow to the brain and makes it more alert. No more staring at your computer, waiting for inspiration, it's a waste of time and does nothing to uplift mood or mind.

For many writers, the best time to think is bedtime. I don't mean staying up all night, just go to sleep thinking about the start of your feature, or maybe the next step, and by morning, it will all come to the fore and you'll be raring to go. Try it, it works, 90 per cent of the time.

Better still, don't begin until the first paragraph is written in your mind, bursting to come out, and if you have done your planning well, the only thing you'll miss out on is the insidious 'writers' block'.

3. Choose your moment

Identify your best writing time, that's when your mind is most alert and you don't feel sluggish or stressed. Some of us work best in the morning, others late at night. Many suffer a bit of a dip after lunch, not quite a siesta, but the brain seems to move in slow motion, dreaming, musing, procrastinating. Use your low time for relaxation, exercise or answering emails, you'll feel better for it, ready to get back to work as soon as the cloud has passed.

Now your turn

- Decide what you will cover in your article.
  Weed out anything irrelevant to your theme or readers and if that happens to be your best anecdote, save it for another time.
- Sort out your ideas into sections, set a rough word count for each one.
  What will you include in each section? You can't cover every beach or theme park, which ones will you select and why?
- Decide on the beginning (your most exciting but relevant bit) and end (your second best).
- Map a route to move with ease from one section to the next.

Start to Finish

What does that mean?

Beginning, middle and end.

Obvious, boring?

Not at all, this is how it works.

Beginning

'Sri Lanka is an island off the south east coast of India.'

So what? Either I know that, so don't tell me, and if I don't, it does not entice me to read on.

The first line of your feature is the most important. Grab attention straightaway and the editor will continue to read, fail to do that and they'll give up within minutes. No point hiding a gem on page two if no one gets there.

How do you grab attention?

Here are some ideas:

- A surprising fact or statistics:
  "Did you know the Great Wall of China has just got longer?"
- An amusing quote or sign:
  "Do not enter a woman" (Bali temple, no entry for women)
- A must-read-on opening sentence:
  "The tyrant's head fell with a thump, just feet away" (statue)
- A close up scene:
  "A freak storm whipped up the waves, the boat pitched and rolled, tall and slim, the perfect shape to capsize in the Gulf of Tonkin"
- An anecdote:
  "All was going well until the bull appeared"
- A topical link:
  "The Prince beat me to it. He got to Bollywood before I did but I doubt he had as much fun..."
- An intriguing start:
  "It all began on April's Fool Day..."
- Humor:
  "Sleeping with 200 monks? Wow, but when I got there, they'd all gone to Taipei, where I'd come from..."
- A sense of impending disaster:
  "The problem is, volcanoes tend to erupt and when they do, you're bound to notice..."

Middle

You've made a great start, you know what comes next, how do you keep your readers interested all the way through?

One magic phrase, 'vary the pace'.

- Mix facts and anecdotes, dialogue and description. Imagine this is a tapestry and you're weaving in a range of colors to create a pattern.
- Change the mood, exciting, quiet, romantic at times or add a little drama or a touch of humor.
- Imagine your writing as hills and vales, highs and lows. If you stay on a high all the time, your readers will get out of breath, sprinkle a few facts here and there and give them a rest. They'll absorb the information but won't have time to get bored.
- Vary the length of your sentences. Every word must count so be concise but within reason, or your copy might end up sounding like a machine gun. It's ok to use conjunctions now and then.
- Avoid hiccups, have smooth transitions: in the evening, later, the next morning, or refer to the previous line, 'the rain had stopped when we reached...'
- Think of your feature as a film, a story, give it movement and variety. Next time you read fiction or watch a movie, do it with a critical eye, see how the scene changes to keep your attention.

End

Avoid repeating what you said, summing up or stating the obvious: readers got your point first time round. If you doubt it, you didn't make it clear, go back and do it. This isn't a school essay or a TV repeat.

You could expand, perhaps giving a hint of what might happen next, or end with a haunting image or an amusing anecdote, or close the loop: referring to the title, the opening scene – start with dawn, end with sunset -, or a theme that held your story together, a local character appearing here and there, a river mentioned a couple of times.

What do you think of these?

"We emerged from the forest, muddy and tired, ready for a snack and a rest, but the young boa constrictor had beaten us to it, basking in the sunlight across the picnic table. We moved on down the road." (Trekking in Tobago, the snake appeared earlier on the trail)

"That night, I dreamed of swirling colors and carpets of flowers and a rice barge gliding under the palm fronds, a haunting farewell to God's Own Country." (Festival in Kerala, the last words refer to the title)

Leave your readers satisfied and they'll be keen to follow you.

Top tips

1. You don't have to write your story in chronological order, start anywhere exciting then use flashback. Keep your opening paragraph around 50 words. A big chunk of writing at the start often puts people off.
2. Bear your readers in mind all the way through from beginning to middle and end. What sort of tone would appeal to them?
3. Remember your photos, close ups and long shots? Think of your feature in the same way, keep to your theme but offer some variety and readers will stay with you.

Find your Voice

"I read your article in… but the first paragraph doesn't sound like you," said a colleague, "it's odd."

I'm sure the editor had good reason to rewrite the intro, but that wasn't 'me'.

Likewise when a feature was wrongly credited (it does happen), my students spotted it straightaway.

So what is your voice?

It's not just how you write.

It's the 'real' you, the mirror image of your life and personality. It's your trade mark and if editors and readers like it, you can't go wrong. It's hidden deep inside, bring it out, trust it and you'll do well.

How do you find it?

Do you have a favorite author or travel writer? Ask yourself why you enjoy their work. Is it the content? Would it be the same if some else had written the story? Probably not. Is it the personality that shows through, witty, humorous, casual, knowledgeable, romantic? Most of all, is it the passion, the excitement you can sense?

You've got it, passion is the key: if you love what you're writing, it will show, if you don't, it will leave the readers cold. Follow in the footsteps of writers you admire, read as much as you can, consider the market but do it in your own way (see *Handy Hints for Writers* by Lynne Hackles). Let intuition be your guide.

Give it a nudge

Do you keep a journal? Read it back from time to time. It won't be polished but it is 'you' and that's what you're looking for. Your journal is like talking to a friend. Some of the best travel writing sounds just like that, with a little gloss of course and attention to market.

Now and then, allow yourself to write for fun. Choose a word or a theme and see what you can write in ten or twenty minutes. Let it flow, don't worry about style or ideas, any nonsense will do. It might cast a little light deep inside you. Do it now, take a break, enjoy and surprise yourself.

Next time you write a feature, read it out loud. Does it sound like you or did you stop to re-read a sentence, a turn of phrase? Maybe that was borrowed and it wasn't you.

Test it

How do you feel when you close your laptop?

Elated?

Confident you tried your best?

Did you have fun?

If so, your passion will shine through, well done.

Remember

Your voice isn't only about telling a story, it's the way you tell it.

Your voice is unique, it shows what sort of person you are, what you care about, how you experience a journey and the world.

Your voice will change over time, as you do, let it reflect whoever you are.

Do it in Style

It's easy when you know how.

Title

A couple of words at the top of the page should be enough to help you focus. If you can think of a good title, such as a pun or alliteration, put it in but don't sweat over the small stuff or use it as an excuse to procrastinate. Most editors like to make up their own titles.

Sometimes, you get a flash of inspiration when you've finished your piece. If it matches your theme, go for it but don't take it personally if the editor has other ideas.

Show, don't tell

Fiction or features, that's the golden rule.

How do we apply this to articles?

This is what two writers might say about a resort:

'There were lots of activities, from scuba diving and fishing to aerobics, beach volley ball, pedalos, banana boats, parasailing, windsurfing...'

'Daunted by the activity board, I headed for the pool and chilled out all day...'

What's the difference?

The first one tells – facts could go in a side box -, it's static, reads like a tourist brochure; the second shows you a scene, you see the writer looking at the board then walking away, you smile and empathize.

So don't tell me how uncomfortable it was sleeping in a tent, show me what it was like when you stumbled out in the early dawn, your back aching, your legs shaking as you headed down to the icy torrent...

Do

- Include details, but be selective, choose those that tell a story or paint a picture: the Buddhist monk with a crash helmet under his arm, the ten year old child mouthing words as she pretends to read like her friends.

- Add a few names, places, people, birds, rivers, trees, choose those easy to read.

- Explain discreetly, what is a langur? Mention 'the langur monkey preening its white beard'.

- Use plain language, especially when recording a dramatic event:
  "Tashi was ten. He lifted his basket, fixed the rope across his

forehead but as bricks fell out, it slipped around his neck. He died instantly. His father arrived within minutes. How much compensation will I get? he asked." End of story. The simpler the language, the more effective it is.

- Use original metaphors, but sparingly, the shivering dawn, the ringing stones.
- Remember the senses, all of them. When you've written the last word, go back and check. No sound, no smell? Think again, they were there.
- Choose action rather than static verbs: 'her red sari fluttered in the breeze' rather than 'she wore a red sari', but don't do it every single time.

Don't

- Use the passive voice if the active will do: 'she was chased by a dog, barking right behind her', 'the dog chased her, barking at her heels', fewer words, more impact.
- Use vague qualifiers, such as quite, rather, fairly, very… Make up your mind, 'it was fairly expensive', what does that mean?
- Pepper your copy with exclamation marks to stress important points, your words should be strong enough.
- Use adjectives that don't paint a picture: what is the 'beautiful' scenery, the 'pretty' girl, the 'awesome' shrine? I can't picture them, can you?
- Use clichés, that's for the brochures, you should do better. Forget the azure sky, the tumbling waterfalls, the blue Mediterranean. The same goes for people, not all Thai are 'smiling', not all French eat frogs.
- Indulge in purple prose, waxing lyrical about the people, the scenery, it isn't cool any more.
- Pad with trivia because you're short of words. Every word, every idea must have a reason to be there so think again.

What could you add that would be relevant?

- Include foreign or difficult words unless it's essential. If you stumble on a word, so will your readers. Keep it simple.

Top tips

1. Always bear your market in mind, what is right for one may not be for another; most publications loathe clichés for instance but a few love them.
2. Don't take anything to extremes, too much of a good thing is as bad for your writing as it would be for you.
3. Read as much as you can, in various genres, and make a list of original expressions, striking vocabulary, turn of phrase, transitions, not to plagiarize but to inspire you. The more you read, the better your writing will be.

Listen to Stephen King:

"If you don't have time to read, you don't have time to write. Simple as that."

Face the Challenge
Suggested answers at the end of this section.

Challenge 1:
Rewrite this paragraph in less than 30 words but keep the main points:

'Our guide was a top expert. She knew everything about the island and could answer all the questions we asked. We were still suffering from jetlag but we listened to every word she said and even when it started to rain, nobody in the group went back to the coach.'

Challenge 2:
Here are a few clichés. Can you be original? You may write a full sentence if it helps.

snow-capped mountains
nestling in a valley
winding alleyways
freezing cold
pouring with rain

Challenge 3:
Imagine you are walking along a river.

Make a list of action verbs, put them in sentences if you wish, banning any part of the verb 'to be' (is, are, was, were...).Think of yourself, the river, the people you meet, what you see and hear, all the senses.

Challenge 4:
Here's a list of colors, can you make them more vivid without using clichés?

Example: red
Cliché 'blood red', better 'earthy red'
Try the following:
blue, green, white, yellow, grey

Challenge 5:
Paint a picture. Rewrite the following so the scene comes to life. Expand if you wish but no more than two sentences for each one.

The mountain views were stunning
The market was full of local color
The train ride was very bumpy

My only traveling companion was a monk who wore an
orange robe

The child played with a sharp knife

Answers
These are only suggestions and if yours are better, that's
brilliant...

Challenge 1:
Our guide, the island's top expert, could answer any question
and despite jetlag, we listened intently. Even when it began to
rain, none of us returned to the coach.

Challenge 2:
In the vast Himalayan landscape, fresh snow softened the
peaks...

Cradled in the fold of the hills, a village beckoned...

Alleyways climbed up the slopes in twists and turns and dark
mysterious corners...

We woke to frozen skies and a sharp crunchy frost...

The rain drummed on the tin roofs, the road, the trees,
blinding...

Challenge 3:
You: stroll, amble, hurry, chat, muse, watch, look up or down
River: rush, tumble (over stones, weir), flow, glisten, ripple, lap
(the shore), shimmer, mirror, reflect
People: jog, picnic, fish, doze, cycle, throw (stones)
Other: twitter (birds), stir (creature in a bush), rustle (leaves),
linger (smells, scents), shift (light), sweep (clouds), drop (nut),
scamper (squirrel).

Challenge 4:
Blue: slate, intense, cornflower blue

Green: acid, apple, sage green
White: sugary, silky white, bleached
Yellow: coppery gold, honey-colored, pale bronze
Grey: dove, steely, greenish grey

Challenge 5:
All around us, peaks rose crystal sharp, reaching for the sky...

Wild mushrooms and garlic jostled for space among asparagus, olives, tomatoes the size of your hand, gingerbread, honey and 45 kinds of sausages.

The train jolted and jerked, right, left, back and forth, no chance for a drink. How far to the next station?

Slumped in the corner, the monk tightened the orange robe around his shoulders and went to sleep. He was my only companion ...

I shuddered as the toddler picked up a 10 inch knife and ran his fingers along the blade. Father smiled, mother took no notice.

And now, the biggest challenge of all...
The time has come for the real thing, let's take a deep breath and put it all into practice, one step at a time.

1. Take another look at your market and make sure your plan is right.
2. Need more research? Do it before you start and set a time limit so you won't procrastinate.
3. Is your opening paragraph ready? Great, time to get in the mood.
4. Wear the silk shawl you bought at the market, light the incense, switch the music on and you're back where you want to be.
5. Write, write, write...

But don't polish as you go, that breaks the flow.

The finishing touch

Later when you have completed your first draft:

- Re-read the section about style and cut out redundant words and clichés.
- Check the senses, telling details and action verbs.
- Look out for repetition, ideas, phrases, small words that tend to litter the copy. Common culprits include 'with, as, while, just, but, where, so', use the 'find' option on your toolbar and take a few out.
- Be ruthless. No one enjoys cutting but it's like pruning a bush, your copy will gain strength.
- Finally, read your work aloud.

Does it sound good? Does it flow naturally? Is there rhythm in your words?

If you need to re-read a sentence or a word, you need to change it.

Have fun and I'll see you in a day or two!

Step 9

Prepare for Take off

"Get going. Move forward. Aim high."
Donald Trump, author

How did you get on?
   Was it easy?
   Hard work?
   Did you enjoy it?
   Are you 100 per cent satisfied?

If you answered 'yes' to the last or penultimate question, you're on your way.

Give yourself a treat, you deserve it, go on a shopping spree, have dinner with a friend, watch a movie, anything that takes your fancy. Don't hurry for before moving on, you must cool off, a couple of days at least, longer unless you're up against a deadline.

Check and Click

What did your mother think when you were born? Most likely, you were the cutest thing she'd ever seen and she glowed with pride. Today your work is your baby, you love it to bits but this isn't the end, you have to prepare it for the real world.

How do you do that?

First, bring out your target market and re-read the travel page(s), but don't rush.

Next, read your feature afresh, slowly, pen and paper in hand, in case you want to make a few notes.

Finally, be honest. Are you sure everything fits? Do you feel, deep inside, that your most carefully crafted phrase or paragraph is out of place, on the page simply to please you? This happens frequently. Cut it out and your work will be that much closer to impressing the editor. Engaging copy doesn't accommodate aimless ramblings or self-gratification.

If in doubt, leave it out

That's one of the most important rules for any writer and it deserves to be on your desk, if not in gold letters, at least in big bold characters.

If the little voice inside your head whispers 'maybe this isn't right', don't ignore it. Double check your facts at this stage, using a variety of sources and if there is any discrepancy, don't risk it. Much better to leave it out than ruin your reputation.

Believe me, it takes only one mistake to be out of the door and if the editor doesn't spot it, the readers will and point it out. Even worse, the word may go round editorial circles that you can't be trusted.

Under the microscope

Examine your copy, spellings, punctuation and formatting. Does it meet the market's requirements? If some words have different spellings, for instance place names, be consistent, use a single source. Don't rely on your computer to point out errors, spellchecks are not perfect.

Many of us find it easier to spot mistakes in print than on the screen. Try printing a copy, going through every page from the bottom up, using a ruler so you don't lose your line. That way, the writing doesn't make sense, you are forced to slow down and much more likely to see what's on the page rather than what you think should be there. Alternatively, change the font or color on your laptop.

Facts can change without warning: ring every number, click on every website.

Finally, ask a partner or a friend to read your feature. They may well notice something you missed, despite your efforts, or they might say 'what do you mean by that' or 'how long did it take to get there?' These are questions the readers will ask but you have not answered. You know your topic but what is clear to you may not be to them. Don't take anything for granted.

No turning back

Is your copy as good as you can make it?

Have you selected and captioned your images?

Is everything else ready, fact box, bio, picture of yourself?

Brilliant, you are minutes away from the finishing line:

- Source the commissioning email (a discreet reminder to the editor) and hit the reply button.
- Prepare a brief letter as outlined below.
- Attach copy, unless you were asked to paste it in the body of your email.
- Attach invoice if terms have been agreed.
- Prepare to send captioned images as requested, thumb nails or high resolution, email attachments –in batches of 2 or 3 depending on file size, drop box or disc (yes, some still like them).
- Ready, no turning back? Hit send.

Sample letter

(Greeting to match editorial tone, as in 'perfect pitch', step 7)

I am pleased to attach my feature on..... as per commission (or in which you expressed interest) and the first batch of images.

I hope you enjoy it and look forward to hearing from you.

Sign

Phone number

Any relevant credentials, website, member of...., but keep it brief

Disaster...

You spotted a mistake and your copy's gone.

What can you do?

Come clean but don't ask a busy editor to find your error, page 3, paragraph 4, line 6. Do your own correction and resend the copy, marked 'final', with apologies.

Likewise, if a situation changes after you've sent your work, contact the editor and offer to correct as appropriate.

Keeping Positive

Don't play the waiting game, it's bad for your morale.

Check your emails as you would do normally and if you feel drained after your hard work, read for a while to clear your mind. You won't even need to reach for a book.

Here's an excerpt from my favorite journey. Sit back and enjoy.

Train to Tibet

One hour into the journey, thirty-three to go and on the world's highest railway, it's fun all round. The young Chinese nurses next door soon join us, four middle-aged adventurers and the only Westerners on board. They're off to Lhasa on holiday. 'Don't worry about altitude,' they laugh, 'we can do mouth to mouth.' The men look at each other but no chance. Any problem and we'll dispatch them to the clinic, carriage 12.

But what can you do on such a long journey?

First it's passport control, then the fruit seller, the piped music, the female guard keeping an eye on things, the height chart used to decide the children's fares, the electronic display in Mandarin, Tibetan and English, recording altitude and 'velocity', maximum 160 km/hr though we rarely reach that. Every carriage is pressurised like an aircraft cabin. Mountains and gorges loom through the mist, green plastic sheets cover much of the valley floor and ghost-like villages pop straight out of the earth. The lunch trolley arrives at 11.30 but we head for the dining car with purple curtains, à la carte and waiter service. Scrambled egg and tomato, pork with edible fungi and boiled rice, we rise to the challenge, chopsticks and all, watched by bemused fellow diners.

Suddenly the train stops, right in the middle of a tunnel, and out of nowhere comes a column of little men and women, wrapped up from head to toes, marching along the track with shovels on their shoulders. They look like the Seven Dwarfs heading home in the dark but fix the problem in no time at all. By 6.00 p.m. the altitude reads 2961 meters. We reach the first prayer flags and snow-capped mountains in the distance. It isn't Tibet yet but you can feel it. Time to celebrate and enjoy our goodies, peanuts, sweets, biscuits, golden raisins. The bags pop like balloons and we feel like kids on a school outing. We munch our way past salt lakes and dunes, sheep, horses and the graves of workers who died building the line. By 9.00 p.m. we are asleep, cocooned in duvets, door locked, trusting the earthquake monitors will do their job when we approach the Kunlun mountains.

All is well and we wake up to a thick layer of snow across the plateau where Himalayan antelopes and black hairy yaks look as frozen as the landscape. We have pot noodles for breakfast and soon the snow recedes to reveal mineral-rich slopes glowing red, ochre and gold above frozen rivers. At 5072 meters, the Tanggula pass marks the highest point and the Tibetan border where a guard stands to attention but the train doesn't stop. Wild geese fly overhead, nomad tents flap in the wind and glinting electric pylons march across the wilderness on their way to Lhasa. A sandstorm dies down as fast as it rose and we follow a near empty road, lined with dummy policemen. There are no scrambled eggs for lunch, too high to cook, we are told, but there is wine from the Great Wall of China.

Wine, altitude? It's a long lazy afternoon then all of a

sudden, a flutter of excitement passes through the train. There are willows and poplars along the river, green patches of land and at last the triple-arched bridge marking the entrance to Lhasa. Back in Xian, we boarded the train at 6.44 on Wednesday, it is now Thursday, 16.44. The Qinghai Express is on time.

Now, let's get back down to earth. Start to think about your next step and in no time at all, you'll be as excited as you were the day you began your first project.

What will you write? Who for?

Think up ideas, study the market, look at your pictures, draft another perfect pitch.

Fine but how about a reply?

"How long do I wait before chasing up?"

Opinions vary but after 2-3 weeks, it's ok to inquire.

Don't phone, send a rude email or launch into a tirade about the merits of your work. Editors have deadlines and priorities like the rest of us.

Be brief, be gracious:

"May I ask if you received the (title) feature I sent on...?

What did you think?

If you need more pictures or anything else, I'll be happy to help.

Looking forward..."

If you haven't heard within a couple of months, don't despair. Editors can be overworked or get sick, change their mind, leave a publication, new staff may have other ideas and occasionally magazines close overnight. That's life. Take it in your stride and look elsewhere.

If you had a reply, that's encouraging, even if it's 'no'. Someone took the time to get in touch, they valued your effort and that's good to know.

Consider the message: what does it tell you?

It's a learning curve

"We enjoyed your work... but I'm afraid it isn't quite right for us."

This may feel like the end of the world but it isn't.

First, re-read your piece and your market. Why wasn't it right? Be fair, identify weaknesses, learn the lesson and next time you'll do better.

Next, remember that list of potential markets you prepared in the early stages? It's time to put it to the test. Go straight to your second choice, study the publication and draft a well-targeted pitch. If the new editor expresses interest, prepare your piece for that market – it will mean a few adjustments or a complete rewrite but it's worth it – and off it goes.

Think of *Harry Potter and the Sorcerer's Stone*, first in the best-selling series, rejected a dozen times.

"Winners don't quit, quitters don't win."

Which one are you going to be?

It's a second chance

"This is an interesting piece but it is rather long for us. If you could tighten it up a bit and cut a paragraph somewhere, we would be happy to look at it again."

You're lucky, maybe you forgot to count the words or things have changed but don't argue, the positive reply shows they're keen. Do as they suggest and you're there.

It's one of those things

"We really like your work but unfortunately, our Sicily advertiser has pulled out but if you have a piece on Crete or the Costa del Sol, we would be interested. Feel free to send other ideas."

What are you going to do?

Reply straightaway, don't wait, another writer might beat you to it.

I once lost a sale by three minutes, that's the way it goes.

It's a sale

"We enjoyed your feature on... and I am pleased to tell you that we would like to publish it in... at our usual rate..."

Well done, you've made it!

You jump for joy, you phone family and friends, tell them the good news, you want to celebrate, have a party.

Great but when it's over, there's work to do.

Business Matters

You've done well, the editor appreciates your work and so should you.

Don't get so elated you forget mundane matters such as rates and rights. After all, you want to make money, remember, and save for your next vacation, otherwise how will you fund and feed your travel writing?

Rates

Publications often pay different rates to different writers, depending on recognition, as this will impact on sales, and original content. Rates of course are also dictated by the publication's finances and range from a few dollars to four figures for a unique story. My top sale was about a 12 year old Himalayan bride whose rape had been arranged by her mother: one mouth less to feed and the under-age marriage legalized by rape. I just happened to be there.

Generally speaking, first time round, accept the fees you are offered and when you become a regular, you may get a rise or in time, ask for one. Should you be asked what you charge, contact other contributors to have an idea.

If you are told 'we do not pay', you have a choice. Accept and think of publication as 'exposure' for your work and a chance to build up a portfolio, or explain you are a professional writer (you will be when they publish) and cannot work for free. You will be surprised how often editors change their mind.

Rights
It's usual nowadays to offer a package, copy and pictures, for a set fee but never agree to sell all rights. If you do, publishers can resell your words and images anywhere, any time and for ever, making changes as they please and scooping up huge profits in which you have no share. Once you've signed up, you can't change your mind.

If you are sent a contract, read it thoroughly. There again, a polite but firm request goes a long way and if someone really wants your work, they may well agree to your terms, eventually. Even without a contract, make it clear you are offering first North American, British, Australian rights or other, and one use only for words and pictures, then you are free to sell second rights in those countries and first rights elsewhere. That's the way to make it pay.

Follow up
All settled?

Excellent, that's a great start.

When your work has been accepted, thank the editor, say how pleased you are then follow up with a fresh idea, but be sure to craft your query as carefully as you did first time round. If you have a couple of suggestions, fine but don't bombard your editor with a list of possibilities. One well thought out idea is better than a dozen half-baked offers.

When your work is published, thank the editor (again), say how good the page looks, how much you appreciate it. Editors are human and partial to praise. If you haven't done so already, or your second pitch didn't hit the mark, send a new idea.

When will you get paid?

In most cases, you need to send an invoice. If you worked on commission, that should go with your copy. If it was an expression of interest, email the invoice on acceptance or as soon as terms are agreed. Don't delay.

Payment dates are usually mentioned at the commissioning stage, 'in the month following publication', '60 days after publication', whatever the company's policy may be but some small publishers prefer to keep their options open. Don't bark at the door within a week but don't wait too long either. Whenever a magazine goes into liquidation, contributors come last on the creditors' list. Not a chance.

Success is yours, how high will you go?

Building on Success

"If you can dream it, you can do it."
Walt Disney

Now you are a writer, there is no limit to what you can achieve. Work hard, aim for the top, amaze yourself.

If someone had told me ten years ago I would shake hands with the King of Bhutan on his coronation or sail with Uros Indians on Lake Titicaca, all thanks to writing, I would not have believed it.

But as you see, everything is possible and the good news is: it's up to you.

Decision Time

How committed are you?

How much time are you prepared to give to writing?

If you want to write when you feel like it or inspiration strikes, that's absolutely fine but expect rewards to follow suit.

My guess is, if you got this far in the book, you are ready for serious commitment.

So let's set some goals for if you don't know where you want to go, how will you get there?

Short term

- How many hours a day or a week will you set aside for writing?
- When *exactly* will this be? Week-end, early morning, evening, on your day off?
- How many features will you write every week or month?

- How many magazines will you read and study in a month?
- How many query letters will you send in a week?

Notice the word 'will', that's a strong word, don't say 'might', 'try', 'could', these are weak, half-hearted words.

Think carefully but don't panic, you can be flexible.

Write down your answers or print them out, big and bright, and stick the poster on your wall, a daily reminder of your promise to yourself.

And the best way to keep your promise is to set aside a few minutes on a Sunday night and prepare your schedule for the week ahead. Good habits bear fruit so do something every day, however brief, to advance your writing: Monday pitch to new editor, Tuesday caption images, Wednesday chase up payment and so forth. You decide what to do, when, and keep to it.

The same goes for deadlines: have your work ready ahead of time and you'll never miss one. You can catch the flu, move house or be called away on an emergency, you won't let the editor down.

Long term
Let's consider where you will be in two or three years' time:

- How many published features in your portfolio?
- How much have you earned?
- How many editors offer you regular work?
- What new market(s) did you break into in the past six months?
- How many trips did you enjoy last year and how many features did you sell on each one?

See it, believe it and you will make it happen.

Nurture your existing markets but search relentlessly for new ones. Publishing is constantly on the move and if you stand still, you will be left behind.

Concentrate on your success but should you tend to forget how well you're doing, set up a few visual reminders. My diary is full of stars, red for published work, blue for commissions, silver for trips and when I want a pat on the back, I open it and smile.

Bare it all on the Web

You can't go more global than that.

Travel writers are lucky. We get out into the real world, discover places, meet people, find exciting stories, then we come home and write, physically exhausted, but we can't afford to curl up and hide in our den. Like any successful business, we reach out to potential clients on a daily basis, show them what we offer and gain their trust. That's the only way to grow. Choose the options that suit you best:

- Set up a personal website. If you're an IT expert, do it yourself, otherwise get help and be prepared to pay. As in any business, investment comes before rewards.
- Alternatively, have a personal page hosted by an association you have joined. That is a cheaper option but you can't choose the design. However, appearing on a professional site guarantees your credibility.
- Start a regular blog or create a site on your area of expertise (as mentioned in step 5).
- Join social networks, twitter, facebook, linkedin, the more the better. Showcase your profile, exchange tips and ideas with like-minded people. Stay connected, be active and available but limit the time you spend socializing.

Any of these, stand-alone, combined or linked, will spread your name, your work and reputation across the world.

What should you include in your online profile?

Any or all of the following, as appropriate:

- Your background as relevant to your purpose
- Your expertise: places and themes
- Destinations you visited in the past two years
- Countries you plan to visit in the next 12 months
- Publications where your work has appeared
- Examples of work (images and copy) or links
- Contact details, links to website, blog and social networks

Include keywords and make your page inviting and bright to attract followers.

Join the Professionals

Some associations have free membership, others not, some have easy requirements (blogging might suffice), others ask for a minimum number of published features per year, all offer opportunities you'd never discover on your own.

Here are a few suggestions:

www.astw.org.au (Australia)
www.satw.org (North America)
www.bgtw.org (UK)
www.internationaltravelwritersalliance.com
www.travelwriters.co.uk
www.travelbloggersunite.com

Join as soon as you qualify, keep in touch with members, meet those in your area, attend meetings and conferences. This is your chance to share tips and news with established writers, come face to face with editors and leave your business card. When you send an idea two days later, they'll put a face to your name and read your mail.

It's also a great way to build your reputation, you're not a 'who is that?' any more, you're one of them, 'the lady with the dangling earrings', 'the chap who writes about...' Socialize, tell a story or two and enjoy the company.

When your name is on the professionals' list, editors might start approaching you with commissions and PRs with networking opportunities from dinners to press trips.

Remember their names and help them to remember you. Create a mini-brand, it could be the way you greet people, your hairstyle or the camera you always carry. Don't go over the top but let your personality shine through.

Lynne Hackles, writer and facilitator, explains how she does it:

> People remember me for wearing a lot of lime green and orange, not necessarily together. And I talk a lot and I am, apparently, amusing. Being no beauty, I've been working on amusing for years. Networking, to me, means making new friends so I prefer face to face as opposed to online. I use the three foot rule, talking to anyone within that distance of me. If it's another writer, I tell them I've tackled everything apart from poetry and pornography, then I go into overdrive. www.lynnehackles.com

Free Vacation, Wine and Spa

A dream come true? That depends how you look at it: press trips are business trips. Hard work and commitment begin before you leave home. You must secure commissions and research the location as you would for any vacation. You won't have time when you get there. When you crash out late at night in five star luxury, you'll be too exhausted even to turn on the TV. Besides, you have notes to complete and images to caption. What time is breakfast? 7.30 but you'll have to get out before then if you want pictures of the castle, you leave at 8.00.

That said, press trips are great but:

Check your intended market: some publications operate a 'no
freebies' policy.

Don't be swayed by the red carpet.

Think of your readers, what would it be like for them?

Who organizes press trips?

CVBs, tourist boards and tour operators looking to promote a
destination, an activity or a new product. They set the program
for a group visit (three to a dozen or more participants).

PRs source bona fide writers through professional organizations, top ranking blogs, websites and networking events. This is
where your reputation works wonders and could earn you the
trip of a lifetime. But don't get too excited. The first approach
usually invites you to register interest and add your name to the
list. The number of potential participants is likely to exceed the
number of places.

What happens if the proposed itinerary does not fit in with
your commission?

You can request an individual trip, at a different time, giving
details of commissioning market(s) and places or themes you
plan to cover.

What if they turn you down?

Approach other possible sponsors, airlines, railways, hotels,
restaurants, through their marketing department. You might be
offered full hospitality or discounted rates.

How are participants selected?

According to commissions which should be sourced before you
apply (except for bloggers' trips).

PRs look for high circulation (except for niche markets), right
readership (age group, interests, budget), suitability for the
theme or activity they wish to promote and the cost of hospitality
compared to advertising.

If you're able to offer added value, you will maximize your

chances. That could be a second print commission or web exposure on a reputable blog or website and social networks. Print and online are the perfect combination, the first targets the right readers, the second guarantees lasting exposure and flexibility when timing is important. Should you mention the web, you may be expected to blog or tweet every day during your visit.

What is it like?

Press trips usually last two to five nights, depending on flights and distance involved.

Most group trips are fully hosted, apart from personal expenses, from arrival at the departure airport. Individual trips begin on location and may or may not cover local transport and meals. Check what is included and what is not.

On a group visit, you follow the itinerary, accompanied by a guide or PR. It's a brilliant opportunity to socialize and network with other writers and possibly editors. On an individual trip, you can request the services of a guide, ask to be left to your own devices or arrange a mixture of both.

Top tips

1. Freelance writers need a commission to get on the list but a commission does not guarantee a place. Can you let an editor down? Not a good idea, especially if it's your first pitch. You may consider funding your trip and recovering the cost through multiple sales.
2. Be prepared to compromise on a group visit, join in the activities and remain gracious throughout. It doesn't do to sulk or complain if you want to be asked again.
3. Dress for the part: business or smart for dinner, casual for activities. Have fun, enjoy the wine but remain professional.

4. Don't chase up commissions on a trip. Editors want to relax and have a good time, as you do. Be pleasant, leave your card then email when you get home, 'it was lovely to meet you' and pitch.

5. Avoid gossiping about other writers (or editors), you might be sitting next to their best friend.

6. Thank your host and PR on your return, get on with your assignment and let them have a copy of your published work.

7. Don't ask for hospitality in the high season. Think low to mid-season and avoid public and school holidays.

8. What do you do if a magazine closes before your work is published?

   You sit down at your keyboard and pitch until your head spins.

   It happened to me and in a blind panic, I approached a dozen markets. How did I fare? Eight commissions, challenging but I had to do it, different angles and more cash than I ever hoped for, ready for the next trip.

Everything is possible

Really? Absolutely.

So here we go:

Find a big colorful map of the world and stick it on your wall.

Highlight all countries or states visited to date, or mark with pins or flags, and count them. More than you thought? How many could you write about?

Now, take a long look at our world, all these places you dream about, the enticing names, the amazing cultures, the mountains and beaches, close to home or far away. Where would you like to go?

Forget about time and cost, just free your mind and draw up a wish list, as long as you like.

Now, decide where you *will* go next year, set a date and make it happen. How? If you really want to, you *will* find a way.

In the meantime, just keep on writing and prepare to live your dreams.

Enjoy the Journey and Happy Landing

**COMPASS
BOOKS**

Compass Books focuses on practical and informative 'how-to' books for writers. Written by experienced authors who also have extensive experience of tutoring at the most popular creative writing workshops, the books offer an insight into the more specialised niches of the publishing game.